CW00742209

MOLTKE'S
TACTICAL PROBLEMS

FROM 1858 TO 1882.

EDITED BY

THE PRUSSIAN GRAND GENERAL STAFF.

(DEPARTMENT FOR MILITARY HISTORY.)

WITH TWENTY-SEVEN PLANS, NINE SKETCH MAPS, AND
TWO SKETCHES IN THE TEXT.

AUTHORISED TRANSLATION

BY

KARL VON DONAT.

LATE LIEUTENANT EAST PRUSSIAN FUSILIER REGIMENT NO. 33 (NOW " REGIMENT
COUNT ROON ");
AUTHOR OF "STUDIES IN APPLIED TACTICS."

LONDON
W. H. ALLEN & CO., LIMITED, 13, WATERLOO PLACE.
Publishers to the India Office.
1894.

TRANSLATOR'S PREFACE.

ALL soldiers must feel indebted to the Prussian Grand General Staff for the publication of Field-Marshal von Moltke's Tactical Problems, and to my former brother officer, Major W. Bigge, of the Military History Department, for the care with which they have been collected and edited. I consider myself fortunate in being able, by special permission of the General Staff, to present this translation to the officers of the British Service.

It has been my aim to adhere closely to the original, rather than to render it into elegant English, which, although it might have been more readable, would have been a less exact and trustworthy guide for the student.

I desire to acknowledge the help which I have received in this work from Lieut.-Colonel John Graham, late 4th Brigade Welsh Division R.A.; and I have also to thank Captain John Marshall-West, 4th Somerset Light Infantry (and late 13th L.I.), and Lieutenant Stewart Murray, 1st Bat. Gordon Highlanders, for kindly assisting to revise the manuscript.

In a small Appendix will be found :—

1. Details of strength of the various tactical units mentioned in the Problems if not apparent in the text.

2. A vocabulary of the German terms as an aid in finding the places on the maps, which are produced from the original plates.

3. Some explanations of the marginal notes on the maps.

When "miles" are mentioned in the text they are to be understood as "English miles," which are equal to 2,000 paces (Schritt) on the scales given on the maps.

KARL VON DONAT.

4, Canning Place, Kensington Gate,
London, W., January, 1894.

PREFACE

(BY THE PRUSSIAN GRAND GENERAL STAFF).

IN order to comply with a wish frequently expressed in the Army, the General Staff has determined to edit the Tactical Problems set by the late Field-Marshal General Count von Moltke during the years 1858 to 1882 in his capacity as Chief of the General Staff of the Army. Solutions are added as far as they could be ascertained with certainty to be those of General von Moltke. Unfortunately this was not possible with some ; to others, however, it was possible to add, besides the General's written solutions, the oral summing up in his actual words, taken down in writing at the time of their delivery.

Some of the problems and solutions naturally appear somewhat obsolete, considered from the present point of view of troop-leading; others offer, according to our present ideas, little opportunity for any divergence in the decisions to be arrived at. Nevertheless, all of them will, on account of their lucidity and surprising simplicity, ever remain model decisions, and afford by their pronounced originality a fountain of suggestion and information.

I.

PROBLEMS.

1ST PROBLEM. 1858.

Vide Plan 1.

The Advanced Guard of a Corps moving from the south on Magdeburg has reached Cöthen.

It is heard there that the Magdeburg garrison has sent a detachment to defend the Saale.

STRENGTH OF THE ADVANCED GUARD OF THE SOUTHERN CORPS:

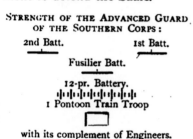

with its complement of Engineers.

Reliable information indicates that Bernburg and the Castle on the right bank are occupied by a Battalion, and that the Saale bridge is prepared for demolition. The rest of the Magdeburg detachment is stationed behind Calbe ; strength, 2 Battalions, ½ Squadron, and 1 Field Battery (8 6-pr. guns). All ferry-boats are beached on the further bank ; the railway bridge below Calbe is destroyed.

The Commander of the Advanced Guard of the Southern Corps requests his General Staff Officer to report :

1. Where on the following day the crossing of the Saale should be effected.

2. In what manner the various troops will have to be employed in this enterprise.

The Saale is on an average 50 paces wide. The meadows are hard, the dykes, partly enclosing them, are only 4 to 5 feet high. The weather is bright.

2ND PROBLEM. 1858.

Vide Plan 2 and Sketch Map 1.

An Eastern Army is pursuing the enemy from Coblenz in the direction of Trier.

At Lützerath it receives information that a Division is advancing from the Maas by Malmedy in support of the Western Army ; it therefore also detaches a Division by Gerolstein, in order not to be disturbed in its pursuit.

The Eastern Division has reached Büdesheim, and from there reconnoitred the enemy behind Prüm. The Tetenbusch was found to be occupied. At the south-end of this wood 3 Battalions and 1

Battery are bivouacking; 3 more Battalions, 2 Squadrons, and 1 Battery stood between Prüm and Nieder-Prüm on the near slope of the Calvarien-Berg, and also 1 Battery at the south-western exit of the town.

The inhabitants declare with certainty the enemy's strength to be:

12 Battalions, 8 Squadrons, 5 Batteries.

Strength of the Eastern Division:

12 Battalions, 12 Squadrons, 6 Batteries.

Disposition for the attack on the enemy's position behind the Prüm on the following day.

3RD PROBLEM. 1858.

Vide Plan 3.

A Western Army is to be assembled at Paderborn.

To cover this concentration and the magazines collected for this purpose, a body of troops, strength as per margin, has encamped in huts near the "Landwehr" east of the town.

ADVANCED GUARD:

1st Infantry Regiment.
3rd Batt.   2nd Batt.   1st Batt.

2 Squadrons of the 1st Cavalry Regiment.

½ of 6-pr. Battery No. 1.

MAIN BODY:

5th Infantry Regt.   3rd Infantry Regt.

6th Infantry Regt.   4th Infantry Regt.

6-pr. Battery No. 3.   6-pr. Battery No. 2.

3rd Cavalry Regiment.

RESERVE:

2nd Infantry Regiment.

2nd Cavalry Regiment.

2 Squadrons of the 1st Cavalry Regiment.

Horse Artillery Battery.   12-pr. Battery.

½ of 6-pr. Battery No. 1.

18 Battalions, 12 Squadrons, 5 Batteries.

The Advanced Guard being pushed out towards Driburg reports that the enemy passed Brakel this afternoon about 20,000 strong, and has gone into bivouac west of that place.

A General Staff Officer is ordered to select, between Paderborn and Driburg, a position in which the Western Corps will to-morrow oppose the enemy and accept battle.

He is, further, in conjunction with the Commander of the Advanced Guard—having regard to the ground chosen and the probable features of the fight the next day—to agree upon the disposition of the Advanced Guard for the night, and the direction of its retirement on the position of the Main Body.

A report to be written by this officer to the Commander on these subjects.

The ground allotted to the various bodies in the position selected is to be shown on a sketch, which need only give a few points of the map for reference.

4TH PROBLEM. 1858.

Vide Plan 4 and Sketch Map 2.

A Western Corps having beaten in the neighbourhood of Eisleben an Eastern Corps, based on Leipzig and of about equal strength, intends to make this victory decisive by the most vigorous pursuit.

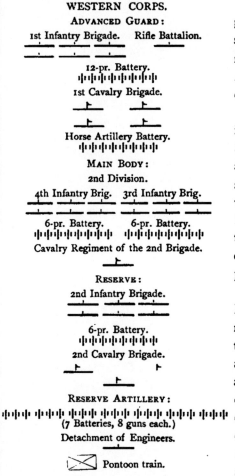

WESTERN CORPS.
ADVANCED GUARD:
1st Infantry Brigade.   Rifle Battalion.

12-pr. Battery.
1st Cavalry Brigade.

Horse Artillery Battery.
MAIN BODY:
2nd Division.
4th Infantry Brig.   3rd Infantry Brig.

6-pr. Battery.   6-pr. Battery.
Cavalry Regiment of the 2nd Brigade.

RESERVE:
2nd Infantry Brigade.

6-pr. Battery.
2nd Cavalry Brigade.

RESERVE ARTILLERY:
(7 Batteries, 8 guns each.)
Detachment of Engineers.

Pontoon train.

Ammunition and Provision Columns.

The 1st Infantry Brigade with the 12-pr. Battery, strengthened by 16 Squadrons and 1 Battery Horse Artillery, is formed for this object as an Advanced Guard.

The enemy is withdrawing by Langenbogen and Schraplau on Halle as well as on Merseburg, that is to say, in the former direction with the main body of the Infantry, the Artillery and the trains, and in the latter direction with the greatest part of his Cavalry.

The Rear Guard of the Eastern Corps offered a good resistance in the strong positions in advance of Bennstedt and behind Deutschenthal, and only towards evening could it be dislodged. The enemy's Rear Guard retiring on the high road to Halle makes however another stand at Nietleben. He remains in occupation of the Dölauer

Heide, and an Infantry column is again noticed advancing from Halle towards Passendorf. Very many vehicles still remain on the road this side of the long Saale defile.

In consideration of the good countenance shown by the enemy and on account of approaching darkness the Commander of the Advanced Guard issues the order that the line Zscherben-Linden Berg is not to be passed to-day.

The Main Body of the Western Corps has meanwhile arrived at Langenbogen, where it goes into bivouac.

The Commander of the Corps is not satisfied with the results obtained by the Advanced Guard.

He orders that the enemy withdrawing on Merseburg is to be followed and observed by a body of Cavalry only, but all remaining forces to be united against his Main Body retiring on Halle.

He requires from his Chief of the Staff :

1. An opinion on what can be undertaken the next day, in order to damage the enemy as much as possible to prevent him from halting behind the Saale, and from concentrating for renewed resistance under the protection of this obstacle ; also

2. The drawing up of an identical order to the Commanding Officers for the execution of the plan determined upon. The weather is bright and dry. Daybreak at 6 o'clock.

5TH PROBLEM. 1858.

Vide Plan 5 and Sketch Map 3.

An Eastern Corps, strength a mobile Prussian Army Corps,* is advancing from Posen towards the Oder, to prevent the enemy from crossing this river ; in any case, to prevent his advance.

The Main Body of the Eastern Corps has arrived at Drossen in the evening of the 12th March, its 1st Infantry Division ; namely :

12 Battalions, 8 Squadrons, 1 12-pr., 1 6-pr. Batteries, is marching on Frankfurt.

At Zohlow the Commander of the 1st Division receives from the head of his Advanced Guard the report that the Laudons Berge were

---

* It is apparent from the problems following and their solutions, that the Eastern Corps consists of two Infantry Divisions (12 Battalions and two Batteries each), one Cavalry Division (24 Squadrons) and an Artillery Reserve (6 Batteries).

found to be entrenched and occupied, that 6 Battalions and some Artillery are bivouacking south of the Damm-Vorstadt, that large masses are visible on the heights behind the town, and troops continually defiling over the bridge.

The report is dispatched at 4 p.m. There are still two hours of daylight. The Commander of the Division knows that the Western Corps is about equal in numerical strength to the Eastern Corps, and only stronger in Cavalry.

What will he determine under these conditions? What measures will he adopt to carry out what has been determined upon?

6TH PROBLEM. 1858.

Vide Plan 5 and Sketch Map 3.

WESTERN CORPS.

1st Infantry Division:	13 Battalions	4 Squadrons	2 Batteries
2nd „ „	12 „	4 „	2 „
1st Cavalry Division:	— „	32 „	1 „
Reserve Artillery:	— „	— „	6 „

25 Battalions 40 Squadrons 11 Batteries.

The Western Corps which is in possession of the Oder bridges at Cüstrin, Frankfurt, and Crossen, has concentrated at Frankfurt, occupied with the 1st Infantry Brigade the field entrenchments on the Laudons Bérge, the Rothe Vorwerk, and the Damm-Vorstadt, and has placed the 2nd Infantry Brigade behind these as a support.

At noon intelligence comes in that a hostile column is advancing by Drossen.

The Commander orders the 2nd Infantry Division to cross on the same afternoon to the right bank of the Oder, the Cavalry Division and the Reserve Artillery however to follow early on the 13th, so that the whole Army Corps will stand behind the Laudons Berge ready to advance at 8 a.m.

A reconnaissance, ordered in the afternoon of the 12th, repulsed the hostile advanced bodies, but finds the position of Kunersdorf occupied by Infantry and Artillery. Approaching darkness prevents an attempt against this position.

Trustworthy reports say that a Division of the enemy started from Drossen early on the 12th in the direction of Frankfurt, but that in the evening two other Divisions* arrived in Drossen.

The Western Corps has orders to bring on an engagement, eventually to force the enemy from his line of retreat on Posen, and to press him against the Warthe-Bruch.

Preceding reconnaissances have shown that the meadows adjoining the Dreist and Haupt Graben are swampy and only passable by bad roads.   The wood on the sandy heights consists of tall pines ; the roads and even the rides through it are fit for waggons.

The dispositions of the General commanding the Western Corps for the 13th are to be given.

Note : The order is to be addressed to the three Divisions and the Commander of the Advanced Guard, and in identical form.   It must clearly show the intention of the General commanding, and yet contain nothing which the subordinate Commanders, who have to execute it, can arrange for themselves.

Just as details are inadmissible, so there must be no statement of reasons.   If such are considered necessary, they are to be added marginally or separately.

7TH PROBLEM.   1858.

Vide Plan 5 and Sketch Map 3.

EASTERN CORPS.

The Eastern Corps, whose object it is to cover the siege of Posen, and which has been unable any longer to prevent the enemy from crossing the Oder, has been marching since 6 a.m. on the 13th on Zohlow, in support of its 1st Division.

The following report arrives from the Commander of that Division :

Kunersdorf, 13th March, 11 a.m.

My left Flank Detachment has been attacked about 10 o'clock by very superior forces from the direction of the Schwetiger Revier (Forest).   In compliance with its orders it is slowly retiring on Sorge, where it is to offer the most obstinate resistance.

Soon after 10 o'clock the enemy advanced with a Division against the front of my position.   He is firing with 24 guns, but still holding back his Infantry.

* The 2nd Infantry and the Cavalry Division of the Eastern Corps.

At 10.30 the heads of the hostile columns, which drove away the Flank Detachment, showed themselves at the exits of the Frankfurter Forst on my left Flank. I have sent against them 3 Battalions, 2 Squadrons, and 1 Battery from the reserve, and have so far prevented their debouching.

Since the enemy, up till now, is nowhere showing Cavalry masses, it may be inferred that they have marched through the Neuendorfsche Forst.*

In order not to get into a situation too disadvantageous, I have now resolved to retreat.

Kunersdorf will be set on fire and the crossing south of it disputed by Artillery as long as possible. The Rear Guard takes post near the wood. If I should be pressed much, I shall perhaps be obliged to cross the Hühner Fliess below the Drossen road and to retire through the close country of Bischofsee.

N. N.

The General commanding receives this report at 11.30 in Zohlow, where the head of his Main Body has just arrived.

What does he resolve to do?

8TH PROBLEM. 1858.

Vide Plan 6 and Sketch Map 4.

The mobile 6th Army Corps is concentrating in the neighbourhood of Schweidnitz.

The 12th Infantry Division, to which are attached the 6th Hussar Regiment, the 1st 12-pr. and the 1st 6-pr. Batteries of the 6th Artillery Regiment, is sent to the county of Glatz, in order to cover the arming of the fortresses of Glatz, Silberberg and Neisse against an enemy, who is concentrating in Bohemia near Königgrätz.

Hostile Detachments near Rothwasser, Nachod and Braunau prevent us from learning what is happening behind the ridge of the Sudeten, still impassable on account of snow. But it is certain that the enemy, about 16,000 strong, intends to penetrate into the county of Glatz on one, or eventually on several, of the existing roads. The road from Braunau to Ober Steine, although not metalled, is fit for wheeled traffic.

* *Königl. Reppensche Fst.*

How does the Commander of the 12th Division intend to perform the duty imposed on him?   Where will he accordingly place his troops?

9TH PROBLEM. 1859.

Vide Plan 7 and Sketch Map 3.

A mobile Infantry Division, strengthened by two Cavalry Regiments, has been pushed out to Werneuchen towards the Oder, to cover Berlin.

From trustworthy sources it is heard there that the enemy crossed that river to-day at Freienwalde and Wrietzen in two columns, each 10,000 strong.

The Division went into bivouac near the farm of Werftpfuhl. The outposts are standing in the line Heidekrug, Tiefensee towards Freudenberg.   Hostile watchfires are seen behind Prötzel and near Vw. Torgelow.

In what manner does the Commander, in these circumstances, think he would best be able to cover the capital?

Dispositions for this purpose.

10TH PROBLEM. 1859.

Vide Plan 8 and Sketch Map 3.

A Western Division : 12 Battalions, 12 Squadrons, 1 Battery Horse Artillery, and 2 6-pr. Batteries, had pushed out as far as Storkow, and is to-day retiring in the direction of Senzig on the advance of the enemy, who has 15 Battalions, 8 Squadrons, and 3 Batteries.   The Rear Guard has halted in Bindow ; the Commander of the Western Division, while still on the march, receives, however, the report that the enemy is following there with a strong Advanced Guard, but directing his Main Body by Prieros ; furthermore, that reinforcements, consisting of 2 Battalions and 1 12-pr. Battery, have occupied the strong defile of Königs-Wusterhausen.

The Commander determines to halt behind a suitable position, and, if necessary, to risk a battle for the covering of the capital.

The bridges at Cöpenick and Schmöckwitz are destroyed.   The low ground of the Fang-Graben* and of the Notte can only be crossed by the existing roads, the other meadows are hard.

* Efflux of the Zeesener See into the Dahme.

What orders will the Commander to-day give to his Advanced Guard? What sections of the ground will the Division occupy? Where bivouac? Where eventually fight?

11TH PROBLEM. 1860.

Vide Plan 9 and Sketch Map 3.

An Eastern Corps is advancing by rapid marches through Cüstrin and Frankfurt to reach Berlin before strong forces can be assembled there for its protection.

A Western Division: 13 Battalions, 8 Squadrons, 3 Batteries, with orders to cover the capital, is standing between Vogelsdorf and Tasdorf, which latter defile is entrenched.

The Commander of this Division hears on the 1st June that both Müncheberg and Fürstenwalde are ordered to furnish bivouac requirements for 10,000 men, who will arrive in the evening.

The reconnaissances, pushed out in both directions, find the Heidekrug and the Hinter-Heide (between Kl.-Wall on the Löcknitz and Alt-Mönchwinkel on the Spree) strongly occupied by the enemy.

What does the Commander of the Western Division intend to do on the 2nd June?

12TH PROBLEM. 1860.

Vide Plan 9 and Sketch Map 3.

The Western Division on the morning of the 2nd June was standing under cover behind Herzfelde. Its Advanced Guard let the enemy cross the Zinndorf brook, and retired behind the Biesel Berg.

When the enemy pressed forward, the Division advanced to attack with all its forces, and threw him back with considerable loss behind the defiles near Heidekrug and Liebenberg. Hostile Detachments advancing from the Mittel Heide against Kagel appeared in the afternoon, but they found this village already occupied. Strong columns arrived in the evening behind the Löcknitz near Kienbaum.

The enemy during the night remains in occupation of Heidekrug, Liebenberg and Kienbaum; numerous fires are burning there and near Hoppegarten.

What position will the Western Division occupy in the evening of the 2nd, and what does it intend for the 3rd June?

13TH PROBLEM. 1860.

Vide Plan 9 and Sketch Map 3.

The Division determined to give up the offensive against the enemy, who having united his forces is now in superior strength, but to observe him still as much as possible.

A reinforcement of 2 Battalions and 1 Battery is moving to-day, the 3rd June, into the entrenchments of Tasdorf.

When the Advanced Guard early alarms the enemy's outposts, it meets with violent resistance.

At 10 o'clock, however, Kienbaum and Liebenberg, then also Heidekrug are evacuated.

A Detachment following on the Müncheberg high road reports the enemy's Rear Guard to have turned from Hoppegarten northward into the Sieversdorfer Forest, and that Neubodengrün was found occupied.

Hostile Cavalry near Eggersdorf prevents our patrols from penetrating beyond Schönfeld. In the evening a report comes in from Wrietzen that a hostile Battalion has arrived there.

What is to be concluded from all these reports?

What further measures does the Division find it necessary to adopt?

14TH PROBLEM. 1861.

Vide Plan 10 and Sketch Map 5.

GENERAL IDEA.

(Holds good also for the next two problems.)

While the Prussian Army is on the Rhine, a hostile Corps has landed at Wollin, blockaded Alt-Damm and detached a force on Greiffenberg towards Colberg. A Division has advanced to Labes to cover the siege of Stettin, which is intended as soon as a second landing has been effected.

A Prussian Division has assembled near Schneidemühl and advanced to Falkenberg.

PROBLEM :

The Commander of the Eastern Division is without any precise instructions at this unexpected turn of events ; he has to act entirely according to his own judgment.

Colberg has its complete war garrison, and is abundantly provisioned. Stettin is weakly occupied, but for the moment protected by its situation on the left bank of the Oder.

From Greiffenberg it is heard that 2 Battalions, 1 Squadron, and ¼ Battery are stationed there, for purposes of observation.

3 Battalions, 1 Squadron, 1 Battery, are near Alt-Damm.

The strength of the enemy near Labes is stated to be 9 Battalions, 2 Squadrons, and 2 Batteries.

The outposts are near Woitzel and Bonin.

The Eastern Division numbers 13 Battalions, 4 Squadrons, and 3 Batteries. For the present it cannot count upon reinforcements.

The Drage as far as Dramburg can only be crossed on the existing roads on account of the swampy state of the meadows; the same is the case with the Mühlen Fliess of the Dolgen See*). Below Dramburg, which is hardly tenable, bridging over the Drage is possible. The Ahl brook is swampy; a strong position with front to the East will be found near Rosenfelde. Labes has little defensive capability, but the Rega cannot be crossed without preparation.

How does the Commander view his situation, and what object does he aim at? Against which portion of the enemy will he turn, and in what direction?

In harmony with these objects the following questions are to be answered.

1. Where does the Division, assembled around Falkenberg, bivouac to-night, the 1st April, and where will the Advanced Guard and outposts be posted respectively?

2. What are the dispositions for the march to-morrow, the 2nd April?

15TH PROBLEM. 1861.

Vide Plan 10 and Sketch Map 5.

The Eastern Division took a position near Sarranzig at noon, the 2nd April, until its Advanced Guard at the Dolgen See could discover the measures adopted by the enemy.

The Cavalry of the Advanced Guard found Woitzel and Bonin evacuated by the enemy, and Labes weakly occupied. It was learned

---

* Here is meant the Dolgen See between Dramburg and Schönwalde, as also the stream running north from it into the Mandelkow See.

that the enemy had left there this morning by the Wangerin high-road.

A left Flank Detachment of the Advanced Guard fell in, at the Vw. Louisenhof on the Sabitz See, with hostile Infantry, which with-drew. A hostile Battery opened fire to cover its retreat behind the Rosenfeld bridge.

Arrangements for the 2nd and dispositions for the 3rd April.

16TH PROBLEM. 1861.

Vide Map 10 and Sketch Map 5.

The Advanced Guard attacked the position of Rosenfelde on the 3rd April, but with the intention only of holding the enemy there in check during that day, and has done so successfully.

Meanwhile, the Main Body of the Division, with the Artillery, marched by Schönwalde on Bonin; the Cavalry by Altkist, covered by the wooded country, drove away, without fighting, the enemy's posts at the Lessentiner Mill, and occupied the bridge there and that on the high-road.

Bivouac in the Boniner Heide* without fires. Labes and the Vw. Kotentow observed.

After dusk the Advanced Guard was withdrawn to Kotentow, the Rosenfelder Mill and the Vw. Louisenhof being only observed by Cavalry.

On the 4th the Division is about to attack by the Wangerin and Claushagen road, when the Detachment against Labes is suddenly and vigorously attacked from that place, and, cannonaded by Artillery, thrown back by superior Infantry and pursued by Cavalry as far as the Heide brook.

What is the significance of this attack, and what resolutions are adopted for to-day?

17TH PROBLEM. 1862.

Vide Plan 11 and Sketch Map 2.

A Southern Army, concentrated between Gera and Altenburg, has pushed out a Division towards Weissenfels to oppose the advance

* Vor-Heide.

of a Northern Army, which is expected from the direction of Querfurt and Artern.

SOUTHERN DIVISION.

ADVANCED GUARD:

4th Infantry Regiment.

Uhlan Squadron.

6-pr. Field Battery.

MAIN BODY:

3rd Infantry Regt.   1st Infantry Regt.

Rifle Battalion.   2nd Infantry Regt.

Engineer Detachment.

Uhlan Regiment.   Hussar Regiment.

12-pr. Battery.   Horse Artillery Battery.

Rifled Battery.

The Southern Division halted at Dippelsdorf in the afternoon of the 1st June. Its Advanced Guard, which has already met the advanced party of the enemy in Weissenfels, drives it out and secures the road and railway bridges there.

The action arising therefrom induces the enemy to get under arms in order to ward off a possible attack. From the high crest on the right of the valley, a Battery of 16 guns is observed unlimbering west of the Kaffeehaus, and 10 Battalions, 4 Squadrons, and 16 guns more are counted on the open ground between Marktwerben and Burgwerben. It cannot be ascertained what may still be in and behind these villages.

After having reported, the Divisional Commander is directed to hold Weissenfels, but at the same time to obtain definite information as to whether the Main Body of the enemy is following its Division sent in advance thither, or is aiming at another point on the Saale.

The inundated meadows of the Saale preclude at present the possibility of bridging; on the other hand, all permanent crossings over this stream are intact and passable for all arms.

What measures does the Commander adopt for the 2nd June?

18TH PROBLEM. 1862.

Vide Plan 11 and Sketch Map 2.

The Southern Division remained at Dippelsdorf on the 2nd June.

The Advanced Guard was strengthened by $\frac{1}{2}$ 12-pr. Battery and directed to maintain the defile of Weissenfels, in itself difficult to force, against any attack.

For purposes of a reconnaissance the

3rd Infantry Regiment,

2 Companies Rifles,

- 1 Company Engineers,
  6 Squadrons, and
  ½ Battery Horse Artillery

will march to-morrow at 5 a.m. by Plotha and the railway bridge above Eulau on the left bank of the Saale.

One Battalion was detached from there to the Nackte Henne (about 1 mile north of Naumburg*). One Battalion went by Eulau to Goseck, the rest of the Infantry and Rifles together with two guns occupied the forest west to Goseck and the corner of the wood south of Dobichau. Between the two the Cavalry with two guns then advanced at 10 o'clock at a trot, round Marckröhlitz as far as Luftschiff without discovering anything of the enemy, notwithstanding the extensive view.

Single officers with well mounted orderlies dashed forward as far as Zeuchfeld, Gröst, and Lunstädt; patrols from Nackte Henne reached Freiburg, yet nowhere was the enemy met with.

At 9 o'clock the enemy had reconnoitred towards Weissenfels and come under fire of the 12-prs., posted at Trompete. He immediately gave up the attack, when disturbed on his right flank near Uechteritz from the direction of Goseck, but kept the mouth of the defile of Weissenfels under the effective fire of a battery east of Markwerben, protected by gun pits on the crest overlooking the valley. Uechteritz was occupied by him at noon; Cavalry and Artillery moved on Obschütz and caused the Cavalry of the Southern Division to retire on its Infantry.

Nothing of the enemy was to be seen in Dürrenberg or Merseburg.

Reports received as late as 6 p.m. bring in nothing new.

The Southern Army moved to-day as far as the Rippach between Teuchern and Mölsen. It intends to advance by Weissenfels.

The General commanding requires :

1. Brief information as to what can be inferred from the negative results of the reconnaissance as to the approach of the enemy's Main Army.

2. A suggestion as to how the debouching of the Main Army by Weissenfels is to be facilitated and secured by the Southern Division.

---

* Crossing of the high-road over the Saale to Freiburg.

19TH PROBLEM. 1862.

Vide Plan 11 and Sketch Map 2.

The Northern Army had sent a Division two marches ahead as an Advanced Guard to secure the Saale bridge at Weissenfels. The enemy forestalled it by only a few hours.

NORTHERN DIVISION: The Northern Division confined itself on the
15 Battalions   2nd June to preventing the enemy from getting
8 Squadrons   across the defile, but while doing this found itself
4 Batteries   threatened on its left flank.

If this attack had been carried out with adequate forces, the Division must have given up its position before Weissenfels. The enemy, however, for the most part, showed only Cavalry, and withdrew before that of our side.

The Main Army arrives to-day, late in the evening, behind Mücheln.

It would be welcome news for the General to hear of the enemy crossing the Saale. He will accept battle in a position near Pettstädt, left wing towards Lunstädt, the right south of Bornthal, attacking which the enemy will have the defiles close in his rear.

The Northern Division is to secure time for the Army to move into the position indicated, without hurry, and after it has cooked.

How does the Northern Division intend to solve its problem on June 3rd?

20TH PROBLEM. 1862.

Vide Plan 11 and Sketch Map 2.

The Northern Division held Markwerhen with 2 Battalions, Uechteritz with 1 Battalion, and left a Battery of Horse Artillery opposite Weissenfels, under escort of 2 Squadrons.

In Marckröhlitz stood 1 Battalion; behind it were placed, as a reserve, 2 Battalions, 2 Squadrons and 1 Battery.

The rest of the Division, 9 Battalions, 4 Squadrons, 2 Batteries, was concentrated in a covered position in Brosig-Grund.

The enemy opened a lively cannonade from the heights north of Weissenfels at 6 a.m. on June 3rd. A Rifled Battery near Beutitz forced at 9 a.m. the Horse Artillery Battery of the Northern Division to retire, whereupon Infantry immediately crossed the bridge. The Horse Artillery Battery took up a new position at

C

the hollow road to Tagewerben, and prevented by effective fire the advance of the enemy until he, on his part, brought up Artillery. It then withdrew on Markwerben, and a hostile Brigade deployed between Burgwerben and Kaffeehaus.

On the right wing a Brigade of Infantry, together with Cavalry and Artillery, advanced at 9 o'clock on the Naumburg road and from the Goseck wood against Marckröhlitz. Guns were brought into action against the village.

Simultaneously three Battalions advanced from Lobitsch towards Uechteritz, but came to a standstill owing to the advance of Infantry on their left flank from the Brosig-Grund.

Markwerben was lost meanwhile, and the Detachment withdrew by Storkau and Obschütz. Uechteritz was then abandoned voluntarily.

A hot struggle for Marckröhlitz, steadily supported by the Northern Division, was still going on, when about noon the heads of the columns of the Northern Army became visible on the heights of Pettstädt. The enemy did not follow beyond Markwerben, and broke off the fight at Marckröhlitz.

The attack was not renewed in the course of the day.

A strong reconnaissance in the evening found Goseck, Dobichau, and Pödelist occupied, and encountered an obstinate resistance.

What conclusions can be drawn from these events with regard to the intentions of the Southern Army, which the day before had arrived on the Rippach and is aware that the Northern Army is still expecting reinforcements?

21ST PROBLEM.   1863.

Vide Plan 9 and Sketch Map 3.

An Eastern Army is advancing towards the Oder in order to reach Berlin by Frankfurt.

The leading Army Corps moves on the 1st March from Drossen close to Cüstrin, and simultaneously occupies Frankfurt with the combined 1st Brigade:

> 7 Battalions, 8 Squadrons, 1 6-pr. Rifled Battery and 1 6-pr. Horse Artillery Battery.

On the news that a Division, 10,000 to 12,000 strong, is said to be already on the march from Berlin towards the Oder, also the 2nd Brigade namely:

6 Battalions, 4 Squadrons, 2 12-pr. Batteries,
is, on the 2nd March, transported across the river above Cüstrin.

The General of Division in Frankfurt receives the order to advance at once on the Berlin high-road with the 1st Brigade, leaving only 1 Battalion behind, to watch the enemy's movements, to unite at a convenient place with the 2nd Brigade advancing from Cüstrin; at any rate to secure the debouching, later on, of the Army by Frankfurt and, if possible, to arrange for its undisturbed advance on Berlin by dispersing the enemy.

In consequence of this the 1st Brigade marched on the 3rd March as far as the neighbourhood of Heinersdorf and is sending its Advanced Guard :

2 Battalions, 4 Squadrons, 2 guns Horse Artillery,
forward on Müncheberg.

The leading bodies of the 2nd Brigade have reached Diedersdorf, its main body standing near Seelow.

Whilst still on the march the General of Division hears that Hoppegarten was reached by the enemy to-day, and that his masses are in bivouac close behind it.

PROBLEMS :

1. What does the Commander of the Eastern Division intend to do on the 4th March ?
2. What orders does he issue accordingly
    (a) to the 2nd Brigade for to-morrow ?
    (b) to the Advanced Guard, still on its march to Müncheberg, for to-day and to-morrow ?

22ND PROBLEM. 1863.

Vide Plan 9 and Sketch Map 3.

The Commander of the Eastern Division withdrew his Advanced Guard before it was attacked. He will meet an advance of the enemy on Frankfurt at Heinersdorf.

The 2nd Brigade is directed by Diedersdorf or Marxdorf, where it is to receive further orders.

At 9 o'clock it is ready in rendezvous position between Marxdorf and the Krumme See, the Cavalry Regiment under cover at the western edge of the Behlendorfer Heide.

If the advance of the enemy, observed by the Cavalry of the

Advanced Guard and distantly visible, happens to be made on the Müncheberg high-road, the 2nd Brigade is to attack his left flank by Behlendorf.

If, however, it is directed by Tempelberg, the Brigade will move into a defensive position from behind the Heinersdorfer See, which position near Heinersdorf the 1st Brigade will hold by itself for the present.

Accordingly, a position is to be selected for the 1st Brigade in the neighbourhood of Heinersdorf, in which it can accept a first attack.

When occupying the most important points of the ground regard should be had to the eventual arrival of the 2nd Brigade in position.

PROBLEM:

1. Show on the accompanying plan the position chosen.

     The units of the 1st Brigade are to be shown as they would stand when the attack was immediately expected, but its direction not yet defined.

2. Show the units of the 2nd Brigade (with another colour in pencil or ink), assuming that the enemy's attack is coming by Tempelberg and that the 2nd Brigade has moved into the position.

23RD PROBLEM. 1863.

Vide Plan 9 and Sketch Map 3.

The Western Division is charged with the duty of throwing back across the Oder the enemy who has penetrated beyond Frankfurt. It is to seize the Frankfurt bridge, which the nearest Corps of the Eastern Army cannot reach under four or five days.

The Division has left the necessary troops at the entrenched defiles of Tasdorf and Erkner, in order to make sure of them, and on the 3rd March advanced beyond the Rothe Luch with altogether

9 Battalions, 8 Squadrons, 4 Batteries.

Meanwhile it was learned that a second hostile body had crossed the Oder near Cüstrin. The strength and nearness of this body were unknown. It appeared, therefore, inadvisable immediately to attack the enemy at Heinersdorf.

The Division, on the 4th March, had pushed out only Cavalry in that direction, and had itself marched to Müncheberg and reconnoitred beyond Jahnsfelde. It became clear that both hostile columns, about 14,000 strong, were already standing concentrated between Marxdorf and Heinersdorf. Until evening no detachments of any strength had penetrated beyond this line.

A Brigade of

6 Battalions, 8 Squadrons, and 1 Battery

has been sent by rail from Stettin by Eberswalde as a reinforcement, which will arrive to-morrow evening, March 5th, at Tiefensee (about 18 miles behind Müncheberg).

PROBLEM :

1. How does the Commander of the Western Division intend to operate further ?
2. What position does the Division take up on the evening of the 4th March ?
3. What orders does the Divisional Commander issue
    (a) to the Division for the 5th March ?
    (b) to the Brigade at Tiefensee for the 6th March ?

24TH PROBLEM. 1863.

Vide Plan 9 and Sketch Map 3.

The Western Division retired on the 5th March from Müncheberg northward round the Rothe Luch.

Favoured by a series of defiles, the Rear Guard has delayed the enemy's advance during the whole day, and only towards evening it is driven out of Wüsten-Sieversdorf.

The Stettin Brigade reports that it will be ready without fail at 10 a.m. to-morrow, the 6th March, behind Klosterdorf.

Till that hour the Division will to-morrow oppose the enemy, hitherto superior, at any suitable point in this neighbourhood, but on the arrival of the reinforcement will immediately assume the offensive.

It may be assumed that the sending of the Brigade from Stettin remained unknown to the enemy, and the Divisional Commander counts upon its sudden appearance, if possible while the enemy is already in action.

In consideration of these circumstances, where will the Division, where the Rear Guard, go into bivouac for the night before the 6th March?

The reasons for the positions chosen are to be based upon the possible or probable enterprises of the enemy.

25TH PROBLEM. 1864.

Vide Plan 13 *and Sketch Map* 1.

GENERAL IDEA.

(Holds good also for the three following problems.)

The 16th Infantry Division is standing at Sirzenich, not far from Trier. It is to defend the Mosel line in order to secure the approach of reinforcements from Cöln and Coblenz.

A hostile Corps has invested Saarlouis on the 1st April, and after doing so is still 20,000 strong.

If this Corps advances straight on Trier, or turns more to the west towards Echternach, the Division will await the attack behind the Mosel or the Sauer, where the ground amply counterbalances the superiority of the enemy. If, however, the Corps directs its advance more to the east, somewhere in the direction of the Lower Mosel, the Division cannot remain at Trier. For instance, the enemy has a four days' march to Berncastel, the Division only two days, but to execute the latter in time it must have sure intelligence of the enemy's movements.

The 16th Division has therefore occupied Wasserbillig, Conz, and Schweich in front of its position. An Advanced Guard is observing Saarburg and Nieder-Zerf from Pellingen. But besides this an independent Detachment consisting of

The 1st and 2nd Battalions of the 40th Fusilier Regiment,
The 1st and 2nd Squadrons of the 9th Hussars, and
4 6-pr. Guns

is sent ahead towards Nonnweiler, to operate quite independently, according to its own judgment and as circumstances demand, in order to ascertain the enemy's movements on the right bank of the Mosel.

PROBLEM:

The Detachment in its advance towards Nonnweiler got as far as the neighbourhood of Hermeskeil at noon on the 2nd April. It halts to cook behind the Dörren brook, occupies Hermeskeil with two

Companies, and is sending Cavalry patrols forward on the road to Nonnweiler.

When at 4 o'clock the Detachment is resuming its march, the patrols return to Hermeskeil, pursued by a Squadron of the enemy. Soon afterwards hostile Infantry is visible at the edge of the wood south of this place. Three Battalions are forming up there, and a Battery is unlimbering by the side of the road.

This deployment occupies a quarter of an hour.

What determination has the Commander of the Detachment meanwhile come to?

How does he intend to act further in the spirit of his instructions?

26TH PROBLEM. 1864.

Vide Plan 13 and Sketch Map 1.

On the appearance of the enemy from Nonnweiler the Detachment took the road to Thalfang, and halted behind the Thron brook, as the leading columns of the enemy followed only as far as Thiergarten.

What position does it take up for the night preceding April 3rd, and what measures of security will be adopted?

What is to be done, if the enemy attacks to-morrow? what, if he does not follow at all?

27TH PROBLEM. 1864.

Vide Plan 13 and Sketch Map 1.

At 11 a.m. on the 3rd April the same troops, which were seen yesterday at Hermeskeil, appear on the high ground in front of Malborn.

A Detachment sent by Bäsch to Hüttgeswasen has surprised there a hostile patrol. The prisoners belong to a body of troops composed of all arms, which to-day is entering Birkenfeld. Reports from the country people confirm the news that several thousand men are announced to arrive to-day in Birkenfeld.

It is communicated from Trier that the posts at Wasserbillig, Conz, Pellingen, and Schweich have not been attacked up till now.

What opinion does the leader of the Detachment form of the whole situation? Where will the enemy advance? Where are his forces to-day?

How will the Detachment act to-day?

28TH PROBLEM. 1864.

Vide Plan 13 and Sketch Map 1.

Can the Division in consequence of the reports coming in from the Detachment arrive in time for the defence of the Lower Mosel ? Can it assume the offensive there beyond the river ?

29TH PROBLEM. 1865.

Vide Plan 14 and Sketch Map 3.

A Western Army is besieging Magdeburg, and has sent a Division, strength as per margin, beyond Ziesar on the 1st June to cover the investment on the right bank of the Elbe.

It is known that 12,000 to 13,000 men are available in Berlin, who were still there at the end of the day mentioned. 3,000 men more had already advanced from Potsdam in a westerly direction.

WESTERN DIVISION:

2nd Brigade.	1st Brigade.
3rd Regiment.	1st Regiment.
4th Regiment.	2nd Regiment.
Dragoon Regiment.	Hussar Regiment.

3rd.   2nd.   1st.

The railway from Berlin to Brandenburg cannot be used in consequence of previous events.

On the arrival of the Western Division in Glienecke, east of Ziesar, on the evening of the 1st June, the Detachments sent in advance to reconnoitre, report from Zitz and Rogäsen that hostile cavalry patrols withdrew by Warchau and Wusterwitz ; from Wenzlow, that Infantry posts were encountered in Grüningen.

A Cavalry Patrol sent forward towards Golzow did not see anything of the enemy.

What conclusions can be drawn from the position and intentions of the enemy ? What can the Eastern Division practically do, to repulse the weaker Western Division, and to break the investment of Magdeburg ?

What does the Western Division intend to do accordingly ? Its disposition for the 2nd June.

30TH PROBLEM. 1865.
Vide Plan 14 and Sketch Map 3.

The Eastern Division marched on the 2nd June from Berlin to Potsdam.

Its Advanced Guard, previously sent ahead to Brandenburg retreated behind the Havel, avoiding attack by a superior force from the direction of Rietz; it holds the Altstadt and the bridge there by a Detachment opposite Plaue.

Numerous watchfires of the enemy are burning near Rotscherlinde.

Rain has made the meadows impassable.

What operations does the Eastern Division contemplate in order to relieve Magdeburg from the enemy's investment on the right bank of the Elbe?

Dispositions for the 3rd June.

EASTERN DIVISION.
ADVANCED GUARD NEAR BRANDENBURG:
Rifle Batt.   Fusilier Batt., Fusilier Batt.

½ Hussar Regiment.

⅔ Battery, No. 1.

MAIN BODY NEAR POTSDAM.
2nd Brigade.   1st Brigade.
3rd Regiment.   1st Regiment.
4th Regiment.   2nd Regiment.
Dragoon Regiment. ½ Hussar Regiment.

4th.   3rd.   2nd.   ¼ Batt. No. 1.

31ST PROBLEM. 1865.
Vide Plan 14 and Sketch Map 3.

The Main Body of the Western Division halted and bivouacked in the neighbourhood of Rotscherlinde after forcing the enemy's Advanced Guard back through Brandenburg on to the right bank of the Havel, in the afternoon of the 2nd June. The Altstadt Brandenburg remained occupied by the enemy; a Detachment is standing before Plaue, and the bridges at both points are destroyed. The rest of the Eastern Division is said to have arrived in and about Potsdam.

The siege works before Magdeburg are so far advanced that any disturbance of them must be prevented. No reinforcements for the Western Division are expected. It is to oppose the enemy where, and as best it can.

The Commander of the Western Division determines to accept battle in the neighbourhood of Lehnin.

How does he dispose his forces for this purpose?

The position of the troops, which remain available for the intended action, is especially to be indicated.

32ND PROBLEM. 1866.

Vide Plan 15 and Sketch Map 3.

A Southern Corps is investing the bridge-head of Torgau, and has repulsed a Northern Division stationed at Herzberg ; it detaches towards Wittenberg, and is pursuing, with a force as per margin, the enemy, who is giving way in the direction of Berlin.

On the 1st June the Corps gets to the neighbourhood of Zossen and east of it. Its Advanced Guard took Gr.-Machnow, and also occupied, with a detachment, the bridge at Mittenwalde.

The Rear Guard of the enemy retired from Gr.-Machnow to Kl.-Kienitz ; large watchfires warrant the inference that his Main Body is in bivouac there.

The strength of the enemy is known. It is known that the 35th Infantry Regiment, belonging to the Division, had marched from its peace-garrisons in the direction of Berlin, and that at the present moment no other troops are available there.

The Southern Corps, under these circumstances, is charged with the duty of seizing the enemy's capital.

PROBLEM :

Disposition of the Southern Corps for June the 2nd.

The reasons for such, if considered necessary, are to be stated separately.

SOUTHERN CORPS.

ADVANCED GUARD :

1st Infantry Regiment.

½ 1st Cavalry Regiment.

1st 6-pr. Battery.

MAIN BODY :

3rd Infantry Regiment.

4th Infantry Regiment.

½ 1st Cavalry Regiment.

2nd 6-pr. Battery.   1st 12-pr. Battery.

RESERVE :

2nd Infantry Regiment.

5th Infantry Regiment.

2nd Cav. Rgt. 3rd Cav. Rgt. 4th Cav. Rgt.

3rd 6-pr. Battery.   Howitzer Battery.

2nd 12-pr. Battery.

Total : 15 Battalions, 16 Squadrons, 6 Batteries.

(18,000 men, 48 guns.)

NORTHERN DIVISION.

24th Infantry Regiment.
64th   ,,   ,,
60th   ,,   ,,
11th Uhlan Regiment.
6th Cuirassier Regiment.
3rd Hussar Regiment.
1st Horse Artillery Battery.
1st 12-pr.   ,,
4th 12-pr.   ·   ,,
1st 6-pr.   ,,
1st 4-pr.   ,,
1st Engineer Company.

Total : 9 Battalions, 12 Squadrons, 5 Batteries.

(12,000 men, 28 guns.)

33RD PROBLEM. 1866.

Vide Plan 15 and Sketch Map 3.

The Northern Division on the evening of the 1st June is in bivouac at Gr.-Kienitz and Dahlewitz, its Rear Guard having been forced out of Gr.-Machnow and having halted at Kl.-Kienitz.

In Berlin, on the quite unexpected advance of a hostile Corps from the south, no preparations of any kind could be made for the defence of the town, such as entrenchments, organising of troops, depôts, police, etc.

REAR GUARD:

Fus. Batt. 64th Rgt.   Fus. Batt. 24th Rgt.

2 Squadrons of the 3rd Hussar Regiment.

1st 4-pr. Battery.

MAIN BODY:

64th Infantry Regiment.
2nd.   1st.

24th Infantry Regiment.
2nd.   1st.

2 Squadrons 3rd Hussar Regiment.

1st 12-pr. Battery.

RESERVE:

60th Infantry Regiment.
Fus.   2nd.   1st.

11th Uhlan Regiment.

6th Cuirassier Regiment.

Horse Art.   4th 12-pr.   1st 6-pr.
Battery.   Battery.   Battery.

1st Engineer Company.

There is only the 3rd Battalion of the 35th Regiment ; the two other Battalions were directed from Potsdam to Ruhlsdorf on the 1st June, and in the evening are there ready at the disposal of the General of Division.

He is charged with delaying the advance of the enemy as much as possible, to allow of troops being dispatched to Berlin by rail.

PROBLEM :

Disposition of the Division for the 2nd June.

The formation of the Division for action for this day is to be drawn up marginally.

34TH PROBLEM. 1866.

Vide Plan 15 and Sketch Map 3.

The Advanced Guard of the Southern Corps in the forenoon of the 2nd June, while actively pursuing the enemy's Rear Guard towards Lichtenrade, was suddenly attacked by superior forces on its flank from the direction of Mahlow, and driven towards Selchow and Wassmannsdorf. The heads of the main body, just debouching from Glasow and the country to the east, across the Fliess, were repulsed.

The Southern Corps soon took possession again of these defiles. The dispersed Advanced Guard joined the reserve, and a new one was formed, which in the afternoon advanced, with great caution, however, against Mahlow ; also a Cavalry Regiment with two guns was detached in the direction of Berlin.

The enemy had retired, protected by his Cavalry, in the direction of Giesendorf. The Advanced Guard of the Southern Corps found the Becke occupied by Infantry, and halted in the evening at Osdorf.

The Detachment against Berlin met hostile Infantry at Neu-Schöneberg, Brauerei, and Hasenheide; it took post for observation behind Tempelhof without being disturbed there. Reinforcements had not arrived in Berlin.

The Main Body is in bivouac between Mahlow and Lichtenrade.

PROBLEM :

What does the Northern Division intend to do in order to prevent the occupation of Berlin ?

How does therefore the Southern Corps intend to operate on the 3rd June?

35TH PROBLEM. 1868.

Vide Plan 13 *and Sketch Map* 1.

Of the 16th Division,
        10 Battalions, 9 Squadrons, and 3 Batteries
are concentrated in the neighbourhood of Trier ; reinforcements are put in motion from Cöln and Coblenz on Daun and Kaiseresch.

The Division is to prevent the advance of the enemy towards the Rhine fortresses, or at least to delay it as long as possible.

A Western Corps surrounded Saarlouis, and with a strength of
        19 Battalions, 12 Squadrons, 6 Batteries
reached Saarburg on the 1st May.

Opinion of the General Staff Officer how the operations of the Corps are to be conducted during the next few days in order to make full use of its present great superiority.

36TH PROBLEM. 1868.

Vide Plan 13 and Sketch Map 1.

The enemy did not attack Trier seriously on the 2nd May.

The General Staff Officer of the 16th Division is requested to report at what point it would be fairly advantageous to accept battle with reinforcements still on the march. In case there is such suitable ground the disposition of the troops for defence of the position is to be shown on a sketch (the scale being four times that of the map).

37TH PROBLEM. 1868.

Vide Plan 8 and Sketch Map 3.

While a Northern and Southern Army are opposing each other in Silesia, a Southern Division advances through the Mark towards Berlin to oblige his opponent to weaken himself by detaching a force for the protection of the capital, which is left without troops.

A Brigade only of

6 Battalions and 1 Battery

is, however, sent off by Frankfort-on-the-Oder, which is to be joined by two Garrison Cavalry Regiments, which have completed their formation at Fürstenwalde and Beeskow.

The Southern Division,

10 Battalions, 4 Squadrons, and 3 Batteries,

arrives on the 1st June at Zossen and Schöneiche. Its Advanced Guard finds Gr.-Malchow unoccupied, but meets at Mittenwalde and Gallun hostile Cavalry, which retires on Deutsch-Wusterhausen and Schenkendorf, where it is supported by Detachments of Infantry.

Bivouac fires are burning during the night at Königs-Wusterhausen, Neue Mühle, and Senzig. The broad meadows of the Notte above Schenkendorf and Deutsch-Wusterhausen are impassable on account of rainy weather.

Taking account of the situation.

What does the Southern Division determine to do?

38TH PROBLEM. 1869.

Vide Plan 16.

A Western Corps, about 24,000 strong, is advancing from Frank-furt-on-the-Main to besiege Erfurt.

8TH INFANTRY DIVISION.

15TH INFANTRY BRIGADE:

Regiment No. 31.

Regiment No. 71.

16TH INFANTRY BRIGADE.

Regiment No. 72.

Regiment No. 96.

Thuringian Hussar Regiment No. 12

1ST DIVISION FIELD ARTILLERY.

6-pr. No. 1.   6-pr. No. 2.

4-pr. No. 1.   4-pr. No. 2.

Engineer Company.

It has not been possible to complete the inundations and the filling of the ditches ; the fortress is therefore at the present moment not secure against assault.

The mobile 8th Infantry Division is assembling in cantonments between Arnstadt, and Gotha, and will be complete there on the 1st May. It is to prevent the advance of the enemy, or at least to delay it.

During the day intelligence arrives that last night the leading troops of the hostile Corps had already arrived on the Werra at Meiningen, Walldorf and Wernshausen, and that quarters and provisions for large bodies of troops have been requisitioned for to-night.

How does the Commander of the 8th Division intend to solve his problem ?

What measures does he adopt for the following day, May the 2nd ?

39TH PROBLEM. 1869.

Vide Plan 16.

The Division concentrated early on the 2nd May in the country around Ohrdruf, and pushed out three Advanced Guards—each consisting of one Battalion of the Regiment No. 31, with two guns of the 4-pr. Battery No. 1, an Engineer party and some troopers as orderlies —on the roads by Tambach, Oberhof, and Schmücke as far as the Rennsteig.

On this latter road the three Detachments were to seek connection, to observe to their right and left, but towards the front, to occupy the defiles of the ascending roads, and to maintain their defence obstinately.

The Fusilier Battalion, however, found the Schmücke already occupied by the enemy from Zella.

On the 3rd May the enemy attacked on all three roads. The Fusilier Battalion was pushed back, and about noon the enemy debouched from the hills at Gräfenroda; on the two other roads, however, he had been unable to gain ground up to that time.

In consequence of these reports the Commander marched with the whole Main Body to Frankenhayn.

The enemy, who here appeared only with a Brigade, was attacked by superior force, driven away with great loss to Ilmenau and pursued, when intelligence arrived that the two other Advanced Guards were obliged to evacuate their position at 4 p.m., and that at 6 p.m. strong hostile columns were debouching at Schönau, Georgenthal, Gräfenhayn, and Stutzhaus. Both Advanced Guards had united behind Ohrdruf, and were still holding this place with a Rear Guard.

What does the Commander of the Division determine upon? Shall the offensive be continued on the 4th May to cover Erfurt, or a defensive position be taken up?

Either for one or the other determination the disposition of the troops is to be given specially.

40TH PROBLEM. 1870.

Vide Plan 9 and Sketch Map 3.

A Southern Army is advancing from the Lausitz on Berlin. Its right wing (the Southern Corps) is driving back a hostile Division beyond Cottbus and Beeskow.

SOUTHERN CORPS.	
2nd Brigade.	1st Brigade.
2nd Rifle Battalion.	1st Rifle Battalion.
3rd Infantry Regt.	1st Infantry Regt.
4th Infantry Regt.	2nd Infantry Regt.
2nd 4-pr. Battery.	1st 4-pr. Battery.

On the evening of the 31st March the Advanced Guard of the Southern Corps has further dislodged the enemy from Fürstenwalde, and has taken possession of the town and the Spree bridges there. The enemy's bivouac fires

3rd Brigade.

3rd Rifle Battalion.

5th Infantry Regiment.

6th Infantry Regiment.

3rd 4-pr. Battery.

1st Light Cavalry Division.

1st Hussar Regiment.

1st Dragoon Regiment.

Corps Artillery Reserve.

2nd 8-pr. Battery.   1st 8-pr. Battery.

1st Cavalry Battery.

Total : 21 Batts., 10 Squads., 48 Guns.

are visible between Neuendorf and the Trebuser See.

Up till now it could not be ascertained from his present line of retreat whether he is escaping pursuit by crossing the Oder at Wrietzen, or turning to Eberswalde in order to maintain himself on the left bank of the river.

In the bivouac immediately south of Fürstenwalde the Corps receives the order to beat the retreating Division if possible before the soon expected arrival of the Main Body of the Army before Berlin ; or, in case it cannot be induced to make a stand, to force it across the Oder, and then to prevent the arrival of fresh troops at Berlin, which are expected there by rail from Stettin.

PROBLEM :

1. What measures does the Commander of the Advanced Guard (3rd Brigade and one Squadron of Hussars) adopt on the evening of the 31st March for securing the crossing of the Corps on the following morning ?
2. Draw up the Orders of the Corps Commander for the 1st April.

The Intentions on which (2) is founded may be explained, if necessary, in a separate minute.

41ST PROBLEM. 1870.

Vide Plan 9 and Sketch Map 3.

The 1st Infantry Division strengthened by Cavalry was charged with drawing off from Berlin a hostile Corps advancing from the Lower-Lausitz.

1ST INFANTRY DIVISION.

2nd Infantry Brigade.	1st Infantry Brigade.
Infantry Regiment No. 43.	Infantry Regiment No. 41.

| Infant. Rgt. No. 3. | Rifle Bat. No. 1 | Infant. Rgt. No. 1. |

1st Division of Field Artillery Regiment No. 1.

| 6-pr. No. 2. | 6-pr. No. 1. | 4-pr. No. 2. | 4-pr. No 1. |

1ST CAVALRY DIVISION :

Cuirassier Regiment No. 3.	Uhlan Regiment No. 8.
Dragoon Regiment No. 1.	Uhlan Regiment No. 12.

Horse Artillery Batteries.

| 2nd. | 1st. |

It is also to secure the approach of the 3rd Division from Stettin to Berlin, which is effected partly by rail, partly by marching by the road, Freienwalde—Alt Landsberg.

On the 1st April the Division, under cover of its Cavalry, continued its retreat from Fürstenwalde, and went into bivouac behind the Gumnitz and Schlagentin See.

An officer sent in advance to reconnoitre reports the ground as far as Buckow to be intersected by swampy brooks, ditches, and hollows, with peat and moor bottom. Isolated knolls, partly with, partly without, woods, offer small positions in all directions, but nowhere admit of the deployment of large forces. The roads are sandy, in the woods, passable only in fours, and everywhere passable for vehicles. The height between Berg Schäferei and Vw. Abendroth beyond this section is cleared of wood. The Rothe Luch can only be crossed at three places on wooden bridges.

The enemy's watchfires are burning between Eggersdorf and Schönfeld.

PROBLEM :

Report in writing required from the General Staff Officer on the most suitable mode of action for the Division on the 2nd April. Corresponding distribution of the troops.

D

42ND PROBLEM. 1870.

Vide Plan 9 and Sketch Map 3.

The last echelon of the 3rd Division : the 6th Infantry Brigade,
Infantry Regiment No. 14

„   „   „ 54

together with the Dragoon Regiment No. 3, and the 5th and 6th 6-pr.
Batteries had already started from Werneuchen on the 2nd April.

While on the march an action in the neighbourhood of Buckow
became audible. The Commander on his own responsibility struck
out to the left at Landsberg, and in the evening the Brigade went
into bivouac in the Stadt-Forst, south of the Bötz See.

The 1st Division retired behind the Garzin section ; authority
from Berlin places the 6th Brigade at its disposal for the 3rd April.

PROBLEM :

What measures are intended for that day?

43RD PROBLEM. 1872.

*Vide Plan 17 * and Sketch Map 6.*

An Army is concentrating near Mülhausen with the immediate
object of assuming the offensive by Belfort.

29TH INFANTRY DIVISION.

57th Brigade.
Badish Infantry Regiment No. 113.

Badish Infantry Regiment No. 114.

58th Brigade.
Badish Infantry Regiment No. 112.

Westphalian Infantry Regiment No. 17.

Kurmark Dragoon Regiment No. 14.

4th Heavy Battery.   3rd Heavy Battery.

4th Light Battery.   3rd Light Battery.

From the Engineer Battalion No. 14.

3rd.   2nd Company.

On the 3rd March the 29th
Division is standing at Mülhausen
ready to start on the following day.

On the 4th March the last
troops of the 28th Division will be
detrained at Merxheim, those of the
30th Division at Mülhausen.

It is already known that on
the 1st March 20,000 to 24,000
French had advanced to Remiremont, who, since then, have been
holding the passes of the Vosges.
One of their raiding parties succeeded in destroying the railway at
Valdieu,† west of Dannemarie,‡
and rendering it useless for some time.

The garrison of Belfort is to be reinforced as quickly as possible

* For the ground not included on Plan 17 *vide* sections Lure 100, and Mülhausen 101
of the French Ordnance Map.

† Gottesthal.   ‡ Dammerkirch.

by three Battalions of Baden Landwehr, and its provisioning to be completed.

The Commander of the 29th Division, who at Mülhausen has at the same time at his disposal 400 requisitioned and laden wagons, is charged with effecting the above.

The Commandant of Belfort reports in the evening of the 3rd March the neighbourhood of the fortress to be still free from the enemy, also that his posts of observation at Giromagny and Frahier have, up to the present, not been driven in.

How does the Commander of the 29th Division, considering all the circumstances, think of carrying out his task?

Dispositions for the next day's operations.

Necessary Instructions (brief abstract to be given).

44TH PROBLEM. 1872.

Vide Plan 17 and Sketch Map 6.

The 1st French Corps is ordered to invest Belfort, and to prevent the arrival of reinforcements, as the siege of that weakly garrisoned place is contemplated.

The 12th Infantry Regiment of the 3rd Division with half of the 5th Battery occupied and entrenched the junction of the roads St. Maurice and Felleringen, in the mountains, and pushed out also one Battalion with two guns for observation as far as Thann.

A raiding party succeeded in destroying the railway at Valdieu.

The 1st Division having detrained at Lure arrived around Champagney in the evening of the 4th March, also the rest of the 3rd Division at Remiremont, the 2nd and the Cavalry Division, with the Artillery, in the neighbourhood of Giromagny. A hostile post stationed there withdrew on Eloie.

1ST ARMY CORPS.

1ST DIVISION.

1st Infantry Brigade.

1st Infantry Regiment.

2nd Infantry Regiment.

1st Rifle Battalion.

2nd Infantry Brigade.

3rd Infantry Regiment.

4th Infantry Regiment.

Artillery.

1st Battery. 2nd Battery. 1st Battery.

Engineers — 1st Company.

2ND DIVISION.

3rd Infantry Brigade.

5th Infantry Regiment.

6th Infantry Regiment.

2nd Rifle Battalion.

4th Infantry Brigade.

7th Infantry Regiment.

8th Infantry Regiment.

Artillery.

IInd Battery. 4th Battery. 3rd Battery.

Engineers — 2nd Company.

3RD DIVISION.

5th Infantry Brigade.

9th Infantry Regiment.

10th Infantry Regiment.

3rd Rifle Battalion.

6th Infantry Brigade.

11th Infantry Regiment.

12th Infantry Regiment.

Artillery.

IIIrd Battery. 6th Battery. 5th Battery.

Engineers —— 3rd Company.

CAVALRY DIVISION.

2nd Cavalry Brig. 1st Cavalry Brig.

1st Dragoon Regt. 1st Hussar Regt.

2nd Dragoon Regt. 2nd Hussar Regt.

Reserve Artillery.

IInd Bt. Ist Bt. 4th Bt. 3rd Bt. 2nd Bt. 1st Bt.
(Each Battery 6 guns.)

Engineer Reserve.

—— —— 2 Companies.

N.B.—The Batteries distinguished by a Roman number are Mitrailleuse Batteries.

From Felleringen intelligence arrives that a hostile Division had in the forenoon advanced towards Thann. The Detachment there took post again at St. Amarin, as the enemy had given up the pursuit.

A trustworthy spy reports from Altkirch that at noon a column of waggons, under strong escort, passed through that place, and is continuing its march on the road to Dannemarie.

It is known in general that considerable hostile forces are assembling around Mülhausen, but that only part of them have reached the left bank of the Rhine.

Opinion of the General Staff Officer on the operations to be undertaken.

(The actual words of the respective orders are not required.)

45TH PROBLEM. 1872.

Vide Plan 17 and Sketch Map 6.

The 29th Division, during its advance on the 5th March, had arrived at Soppe le Bas before noon, when from the Advanced Guard which had approached La Chapelle, intelligence came in that the Cavalry, reconnoitring towards St. Germain, had come under Infantry fire from that place, and that very strong columns of all arms were advancing by Anjoutey.

The Detachment escorting the convoy of wagons on the exposed flank reports that it has taken up a position in front of Bessoncour against bodies of the enemy's Cavalry, and that the convoy was approaching Belfort unmolested.

In these circumstances the General of Division determined not to expose himself to an attack by superior numbers.

The Main Body took the road south to Traubach ; the Right Flank Detachment, ordered back from Soppe le Haut, followed, and the Advanced Guard covered this movement by marching parallel along the east bank of the St. Nicolas brook, and by occupying the bridges over it. When the enemy about noon advanced *en masse* from St. Germain and Menoncourt against La Rivière and Fontane, it began to retreat, now as a Rear Guard, skirmishing in the direction of Traubach.

The Main Body of the enemy did not cross the brook ; only the Cavalry proceeded beyond it.

The Rear Guard of the Division, therefore, continued to hold Bréchaumont and Bois d'Elbach ; the Division bivouacked near Traubach.

Early on the 6th March there are standing :

The 28th Division at Cernay,*

The 30th Division with the Corps Artillery of the 14th Army Corps at Mülhausen ready for action, and with the 29th Division placed under joint command of the General commanding the 14th Army Corps ; a Cavalry Division is formed of four available regi-ments. The further concentration of troops at Mülhausen is to be covered towards the west, and the investment of Belfort to be pre-vented.

Instructions of the General commanding to three Generals of Division for the 6th March ?

---

* Sennheim.

46TH PROBLEM. 1873.

Vide Plan 18 and Sketch Map 3.

After an unsuccessful action on the right bank of the Oder :
The 2nd Army Corps retired on Cüstrin, the 5th Infantry Division on Frankfurt. The enemy followed in both directions with superior forces.

5TH INFANTRY DIVISION.
9th Infantry Brigade.
Infantry Regiment No. 48.

Life Grenadier Regiment No. 8.

10th Infantry Brigade.
Infantry Regiment No. 52.

Grenadier Regiment No. 12.

Rifle Battalion No. 3.

Dragoon Regiment No. 12.

Field Artillery Division.
(4 Batteries, 6 guns each.)
Engineer Company.

The 2nd Army Corps, on the 1st March, took up a position at the edge of the valley, in front of Seelow, and is observing the river above the fortress as far as Reitwein.

The 5th Infantry Division was driven out of Frankfurt in the afternoon of the same day, the bridge could only be partly destroyed. The Advanced Guard of the enemy occupied Boosen and is scouring the country this evening as far as Trepplin and Sieversdorf.

The Division bivouacs during the night near Petershagen.

At the present moment we have no other forces in or around Berlin.

How and where does the Commander of the 5th Division intend to offer resistance to the enemy's further advance ?

47TH PROBLEM. 1873.

Vide Plan 18 and Sketch Map 3.

Show on the map a "position of readiness" in which to receive on the 2nd March an attack by the enemy west of the Falkenhagen line of lakes.

48TH PROBLEM. 1873.

Vide Plan 18 and Sketch Map 3.

The 2nd Army Corps could only in the course of the 2nd March complete defiling through Cüstrin and is standing at Seelow.

The 8th Infantry Brigade, strengthened by the 5th Hussars and a Battery, occupied Dolgelin, and is patrolling to Reitwein, Podelzig, and Karzig. Small bodies of the enemy were seen in the neighbourhood of Lebus. A post of observation at Reitwein was, however, not attacked, and did not notice any preparations for building a bridge above Cüstrin.

It is reported from Frankfurt that the bridge there is very much damaged, and that the enemy is constructing a military bridge leading to the Lebuser Vorstadt.

Before Cüstrin, on the Kietzer Wiesen, detachments of the enemy were seen, which, however, kept out of range. The extensive watch-fires, which were burning during the night preceding the 2nd of March in the country about Sonnenburg, are no more seen to-night.

The 5th Infantry Division, which early on the 2nd took up a position, Falkenhagen-Arensdorf, reports that it had not been attacked there. Its Rear Guard at Trepplin, it is true, was frequently alarmed ; had indeed been pushed back behind the lake defile, but was able to occupy the village again in the evening.

Large bivouacs of the enemy are seen near Boosen, Wüst-Kunersdorf, and Rosengarten.

Dispositions of the General commanding the 2nd Army Corps for all three Divisions for the 3rd March.

49TH PROBLEM. 1874.

Vide Plan 19.

At the Grand Headquarters of His Majesty in Pont-à-Mousson reports came in on the 16th August up to 5 o'clock in the afternoon according to which the 3rd and 10th Corps were apparently engaged with the French Main Army west of Metz, and only with great difficulty able to maintain themselves.

Of the 2nd Army on the evening this day :

The 2nd Corps got as far as Buchy, nine miles south of Metz, after very long marches.

The 4th Corps stood at Les Saizerais, Advanced Guard against Toul ;

The Guard Corps : headquarters, Bernecourt ; Advanced Guard, Rambucourt; the Uhlan Brigade pushed out towards Commercy—St. Mihiel;

The 12th Corps was about Pont-à-Mousson, head-quarters, Fey en Haye; Advanced Guard, Regniéville en Haye; the 12th Cavalry Division at Vigneulles;

The 9th Corps was still partly on the right bank of the Moselle, but with its leading troops as far as the battlefield.

Of the 1st Army:

The 1st Corps had to remain opposite Metz for obser-vation, and to secure the communications in rear;

The 7th and 8th Corps, on the other hand, had already moved up to Corny and Arry on the Moselle respectively, in order to cross the river next day on the bridges existing there, but only after the 9th Corps.

Prince Friedrich Karl was on the battlefield; his quarters for the night were not known; those of General v. Steinmetz were at Coin sur Seille.

A Field Telegraph was established to Fey en Haye and Berne-court.

PROBLEM:

On the 17th of August those Corps which, in the course of the day can reach the battlefield, are to be moved up as early as possible. The left wing at Mars la Tour is, above all, to be reinforced. Cavalry to be pushed out from there towards the roads from Metz to Etain and Briey.

Toul continues to be observed, but towards the Maas only the Guard Uhlan Brigade remains in observation.

The two available Corps of the 1st Army are to be brought up by the shortest road to the right wing of the position at Vionville.

All crossing and blocking of the Corps ordered up are to be avoided. The supply of ammunition must not be forgotten.

Direct reports to His Majesty are to be sent to the height south of Flavigny.

Issue of the orders for the 17th of August at the Grand Head-quarters, Pont-à-Mousson, at 7 p.m. of the 16th as far as practicable by wire, and as far as necessary directly to the Corps Commanders, communicating at the same time to the Army Commanders what has been ordered.

At the end of the telegrams the number of words is to be noted (exclusive of address and signature).

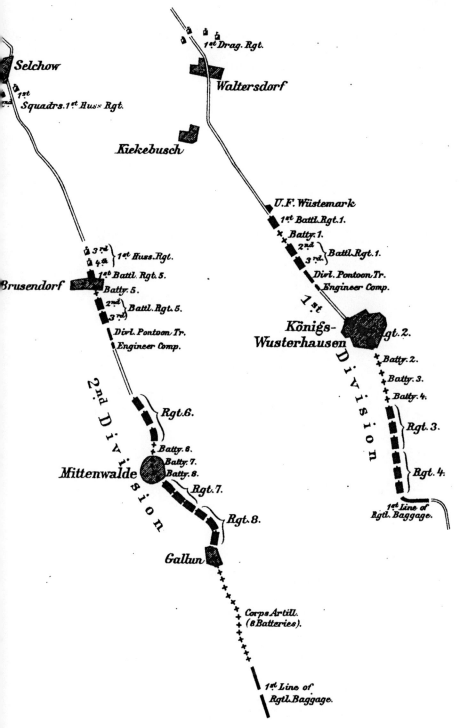

Selchow

1st Drag. Rgt.

Waltersdorf

2nd 1st
Squadrs. 1st Huss Rgt.

Kiekebusch

U.F. Wüstemark

1st Battl. Rgt. 1.

Batty. 1.

2nd
3rd } Battl. Rgt. 1.

Divl. Pontoon Tr.

Engineer Comp.

3rd
4th } 1st Huss. Rgt.

1st Battl. Rgt. 5.

Brusendorf

Batty. 5.

2nd
3rd } Battl. Rgt. 5.

Divl. Pontoon Tr.

Engineer Comp.

Königs-
Wusterhausen

Rgt. 2.

Batty. 2.

Batty. 3.

Batty. 4.

1st Division

2nd Division

Rgt. 6.

Batty. 6.
Batty. 7.
Batty. 8.

Mittenwalde

Rgt. 7.

Rgt. 8.

Rgt. 3.

Rgt. 4.

1st Line of
Rgtl. Baggage.

Gallun

Corps Artill.
(8 Batteries).

1st Line of
Rgtl. Baggage.

lag d. Kgl. Hofbuchh. v. E. S. Mittler & Sohn, Berlin. (Kochstr. 68/70.)   Geogr. lith. Inst. u. Steindr. v. Wilhelm Greve, Berlin.

50TH PROBLEM. 1874.

Vide Plan 20 and Sketch Map 7.

On the intelligence that a hostile Corps is advancing from Wirballen on Königsberg, the Prussian 1st Army Corps is detached by Lötzen and charged with preventing the further advance of the enemy, and throwing him back, if possible, across the frontier.

The Prussian Corps, for this purpose, has been strengthened by the 1st and 2nd Cavalry Divisions (32 Squadrons and 2 Batteries Horse Artillery). It arrives to-night at Darkehmen—Advanced Guard near Dinglauken—and learns that the enemy is standing near Stallupönen.

What measures are intended for to-morrow?

———————

51ST PROBLEM. 1875.

Vide Plan 8 and Sketch Map 3.

An Army Corps is advancing from the Lausitz on Berlin.

The enemy, for the protection of his capital, is said to have concentrated forces in the neighbourhood of Eberswalde; it is not known in what strength and how far he has already advanced towards us.

The Corps is to obtain definite information about this; therefore to act as much as possible offensively, but against superior numbers, which are probable, it is to seek to maintain itself until the arrival of reinforcements.

On the 1st of March the Corps is advancing in the order of march as given on the opposite page, with the 1st Division by Königs-Wusterhausen, with the 2nd by Mittenwalde. The heads of both Main Bodies have crossed the Notte Fliess and its bogs when the following reports come in from the Advanced Guards:

1. *Advanced Guard of the 2nd Division.*

Brusendorf, 1st March, 10 a.m.

Advanced Cavalry reports from Selchow that its scouts found Wassmannsdorf and Klein Ziethen not occupied by the enemy.

2. *Advanced Guard of the 1st Division.*

Unter-Försterei Wüstemark, 1st March, 10 a.m.

The Dragoons received Artillery fire in the neighbourhood of the Schönfelder See from the direction of Rudow.

Right flank patrol found Bohnsdorf occupied by Infantry. Hostile Cavalry is debouching from Glienicke, ours retiring towards Waltersdorf. I have provisionally ordered . . . . .

PROBLEM :

1. What measures will the Commander of the Advanced Guard of the 1st Division on his own initiative have adopted and reported ?
2. How does the Corps Commander intend to solve his problem ?

52ND PROBLEM. 1875.

Vide Plan 8 and Sketch Map 3.

On the 1st March the 2nd Army Corps began crossing the Spree early in the morning, making use of the Cöpenick bridge, of a pontoon bridge north-east of Marienthal, and of the railway bridge at Stralow.

6TH DIVISION.
11th Infantry Brigade.
Regiment No. 20.
    „   „ 35.
12th Infantry Brigade.
Regiment No. 24.
    „   „ 64.
Hussar Regiment No. 3.
1st Division Field Artillery Regt. No. 18.
1st, 2nd, 3rd, 4th Batteries.

The 3rd Dragoon Regiment was pushed out beyond Glienicke for observation of the enemy, and in order to secure its debouching, Bohnsdorf was provisionally occupied by Infantry in small force.

Reports showed that the enemy was advancing on the roads by Königs-Wusterhausen and Mittenwalde, and at 9.30 Cavalry detachments of his showed themselves this side of Waltersdorf.

At that time the Corps was in rendezvous formations behind the line, Rudow—Gr. Ziethen.

The 6th Infantry Division, together with the 6th Cavalry Brigade, has been detailed as a reinforcement for the Corps, but can only start at 9 a.m. from behind Tempelhof.

1. What instructions does the Commander of the 2nd Army Corps give to the leader of the 6th Division ?
2. How does the latter, according to these instructions, arrange his advance ? Direction and order of march are to be sketched with the aid of the map.

53RD PROBLEM. 1876.

Vide Plan 7 and Sketch Map 3.

The mobile 5th Infantry Division has orders to march without delay from Frankfurt-on-the-Oder by Biesenthal to Zehdenick.

5TH INFANTRY DIVISION.

10th Brigade.	9th Brigade.
Infantry Regt. No. 52.	Infantry Regt. No. 48.
Grenadier Regt. No. 12.	Grenadier Regt. No. 8.

Dragoon Regiment No. 12.

1st Division Field Artillery Regiment No. 18.
(24 guns.)
Trains.

The Main Body of the Division reached Biesenthal on the evening of the 1st September and went into bivouac around that place. The Advanced Guard has pushed to Lanke. On the rumour that during the day strong bodies of hostile troops had been transported on the Stettin railway from Berlin to Bernau, the 1st Squadron of the Dragoons was sent to reconnoitre. It met Cavalry patrols of the enemy near Rüdnitz, who retired on Ladeburg, which place was found to be occupied by Infantry.

What measures does the Divisional Commander adopt by reason of these reports?

54TH PROBLEM. 1876.

Vide Plan 21 and Sketch Map 8.

A Southern Division is marching from Neidenburg on Osterode. To protect that place a Northern Division has taken up a position in advance of it.

SOUTHERN DIVISION.

2nd Brigade.	1st Brigade.
3rd Regiment.	1st Regiment.
4th Regiment.	2nd Regiment.

3rd Cavalry Brigade.

Uhlan Regiment.	Hussar Regiment.

Horse Artillery Battery.

3rd Artillery Brigade.
(32 guns.)

The Southern Division has arrived near Hohenstein in the evening of the 1st, and has gone into bivouac there. Cavalry patrols, sent in advance, encountered Infantry posts of the enemy at Osterwein and Gross-Gröben.

What measures does the Commanding Officer of the Southern Division adopt for the advance on the following day?

55TH PROBLEM. 1877.

Vide Plan 4 and 11 and Sketch Map 2.

The mobile 8th Division is marching from Erfurt by Eckartsberga to join the 4th Army Corps assembling near Eisleben.

8TH INFANTRY DIVISION.

16th Infantry Brig.	15th Infantry Brig.
Regiment No. 96.	Regiment No. 71.
Regiment No. 72.	Regiment No. 31.

Rifle Battalion No. 4.

Hussar Regiment No. 12.

2nd Division Field Artillery Regt. No. 4.

Engineer Company.

Trains.

As the advance of a superior hostile Division is expected from the direction of the Saale, a Flank Detachment of all arms is moved on the 1st of March by St. Micheln and Eichstädt in order to secure the march from Freiburg to Querfurt. The trains are ordered to take the road on the right bank of the Unstrut as far as Nebra and from there to Ziegelroda.

About midday the Commander at Steigra receives the report from the Commander of the Detachment that strong columns are advancing from Merseburg by the high-road to Lauchstädt, and by the road to Clobicau, and that he intended for the present to halt between Eichstädt and Schafstädt in order to observe.

What measures does the General of Division adopt for the evening of the 1st and for the continuation of the march on the 2nd March?

56TH PROBLEM. 1877.

Vide Plan 4 and 11 and Sketch Map 2.

The 4th Army Corps: 25 Battalions, 30 Squadrons, 17 Batteries. and the 12th „ 26 „ 30 „ 18 „ are to practise Field Manœuvres against each other.

TIME TABLE.

4th September, Rest.

| 5th | „ | Review. | } of the 4th or 12th Corps. |
| 6th | „ | Corps manœuvre | |

| 7th | „ | Review. | } of the 12th or 4th Corps. |
| 8th | „ | Corps manœuvre | |

9th „ Sunday rest.

10th	„	} Field manœuvre of both Corps.
11th	„	
12th	„	

During the preliminary exercises the cantonments of the 4th Corps extend east as far as the line Schraplau-Steigra, those of the 12th Corps west as far as the frontier, near Markranstädt and Pegau.

An officer is sent to select on the spot a favourable locality for the manœuvres.

After determining upon this he is requested to draw up:

1. A General Idea, which will hold good for all three days of the exercise.
2. A Special Idea for the first day, and for each individual Corps.
3. To indicate suitable depôts for bivouac requisites.
4. To define the limits of the cantonments of the opposing forces for the day of rest on the 9th of September.

REMARKS ON THE PLANNING OF MANŒUVRES.

At the three days' Field Manœuvres of two Army Corps against each other it has to be considered that during the concentration of large bodies of troops every day causes a very considerable outlay.

The time table, fixed by superior authority, provides that the days of rest necessary for the troops fall, as far as is practicable, on the Sundays, and particularly that the Field Manœuvres are not interrupted by a Sunday or holiday.

For the same economic reasons the two Corps concerned will not hold their divisional manœuvres at too great a distance from each other, in order to avoid long marches. It is inadmissible that one Corps should have more than one day's rest because the other is still marching.

The ground for the Field Manœuvres will, therefore, as a rule, have to be chosen somewhere between the cantonments in which the preliminary manœuvres of both come to an end. It is obvious that a longer march can be given to that Corps which soonest concludes those preliminary manœuvres.

For the day of rest before the beginning of the Field Manœuvres the districts of the cantonments of both Corps are to be separated from each other, and the rendezvous is to be determined in such a manner that the parties, or at least their Advanced Guards, shall actually meet on the first day.

The rearmost limits of these cantonments are determined by the length of march which is permissible from the most distant quarters to the place of rendezvous. The interests of the Home Office in this matter generally clash with those of the War Office, as the former demands extended cantonments, in order to ease the landlords ; the latter limited ones in order to spare the physical strength of the men in quarters.

The rendezvous must, therefore, not be chosen too far from the centre of the cantonments in order that the Infantry may not have to march to it more than about 7 miles.

With those restrictions such ground is now to be looked for as most favours the deployment and effect of all arms. We will have to avoid insurmountable obstacles and also the too frequent village fights, which can only be imperfectly represented in manœuvres.

According to the ground selected, a General Idea, holding good for all three days, is then sketched, and at the same time a Special Idea for each Corps for the first day of the exercise.

The General Idea indicates the supposed conditions of war under which the two Corps oppose each other. Each of them must be able to gather from that Idea where the Corps has come from, what is required of it, whether and where it might eventually find support, and what is known of the enemy. The drawing up of the General Idea demands the greatest care. It must not contain far-fetched strategical suppositions, or anything which by the nature of the thing can only be known to one of the two parties. It must be precisely worded and admit of no doubts ; it must be complete, and yet brief. A General Idea, well thought out, will always admit of being compressed into a few lines.

All that can be known to one party only, and is necessary for it to know : more precise instructions, intelligence about advance of reinforcements, reports on the position of the enemy's outposts, etc., belong to the Special Idea.

The Special Idea must not restrict freedom of action when once the situation is stated. It is a mistake to say, "The Commander determines," or " The Division occupies," etc. All that must be entirely left to the leaders of the troops, and from this it follows that at the outset the Special Idea can only be settled for the first day of the manœuvre. In a note the rendezvous for the Main Body is stated, and the hour at which the movements of the troops may begin. The next Special Ideas are regulated by the course of the day's events.

But it still remains necessary at the same time to keep the progress of a peace manœuvre in a certain preconceived direction, in order to make use of the most instructive ground, to bring about interesting phases of battle, to feed the troops during the exercise, and to facilitate their return to their garrison at the conclusion of it.

The superior commanders have sufficient means of preventing the several parties from striking into quite a different direction from that intended, *e.g.*, strengthening one party by Battalions indicated by flags, intelligence about the enemy, even an order changing the original intention, but all those means are to be derived without doing violence to the General Idea, and must be considered beforehand when forming it.

The course of the whole exercise, as judged by probabilities, gives a clue for indicating beforehand to the Corps Commissariat the points for storing the bivouac requisites.

Large villages are to be chosen for them in which suitable buildings can be hired and teams be sheltered, such villages being close to the probable bivouac, but outside the field of action.

57TH PROBLEM.　1878.

Vide Plan 22.

A Cavalry Brigade is observing our frontier from Verny. It is holding with dismounted men the bridges of the Seille from Marly to Cheminot, which is at this time of the year unfordable. Its patrols are scouring the country unmolested as far as the wooded heights on the right bank of the Moselle, but they find these occupied by the Infantry of the enemy, so that no view can be obtained of the ground beyond them.

CAVALRY BRIGADE.

2nd and 1st Uhlan Regiments.

2nd and 1st Dragoon Regiments.

Horse Artillery Battery.

RESERVE DIVISION.

4th and 3rd Infantry Regiments.

2nd and 1st Infantry Regiments.

1st Hussar Regiment.

4th, 3rd, 2nd, and 1st Batteries.

The bridge at Ars-sur-Moselle is occupied by troops from Metz, and thence also provision has been made to guard the railway itself to Saarbrücken against small raiding parties of the enemy.

During the 1st May a Reserve Division detrained at Courcelles to complete the garrison of Metz, but for the present is charged with protecting the most exposed part of the line from Courcelles to Han against extensive enterprises of the enemy.

The Cavalry Brigade is placed under the command of the General of Division.

It reports that up to the evening of the 1st May its posts on the Seille had not been disturbed by the enemy.

1. How does the General Commanding propose to solve his problem?
2. What are his first measures?

58TH PROBLEM. 1878.

Vide Plan 22.

The Division on the 1st May had taken up its quarters in advance of Courcelles as far as Mécleuves and Silly, whence it moved forward in two columns to the Seille on the 2nd May.

The 1st Brigade on the right detached the 1st Battalion of the 1st Infantry Regiment with a Battery straight to Pouilly, and marched by Orny and Verny, where the 2nd Battalion of the 1st Regiment remained, with one Squadron and the 2nd Battery, behind Louvigny. To the latter place, also, the 2nd Brigade advanced by Vigny. The Cavalry Brigade was ordered to march to Vigny by way of Goin. The

10 Battalions, 19 Squadrons, 3 Batteries

thus concentrated near Louvigny in the forenoon, entrenched themselves there at once in a position in advance of the road, Verny—Raucourt.

On the 3rd May, before noon, a hostile column showing

6 Battalions, 8 Squadrons, 2 Batteries

advances from Corny against Coin les Cuvry, and shells without success our posts standing under cover on the right bank of the Seille.

Repeated attempts to bring Infantry and bridging material forward to the river, the bridges of which are destroyed and guarded, fail on account of the fire of the Battery on the height 203 west of Pouilly, and of the skirmishers south of that place and in the patches of wood west of Verny.

The enemy has advanced with considerably stronger forces from Pont-à-Mousson by Les Menils. He is deploying Artillery to the left near Longeville and to the right on the height 224, and soon after advances with Infantry against both road bridges, which are only barricaded and weakly occupied. Our post of observation is withdrawing, not without some loss, in the valley on Louvigny.

The enemy occupies Cheminot, but during his further advance he comes under the fire of our three Batteries, opposite to which he is unable to deploy with any advantage an equal number on the height 216. The village catches fire and the enemy retires behind the slope to the Moselle.

A somewhat lengthy pause occurs in the action, and not before the afternoon are large dust clouds observed in a southerly direction. The 1st Uhlan Regiment, which trots forward by Allémont, repulses near Raucourt a hostile flank detachment, and discovers from the height 238 the advance, by Port sur Seille on Nomeny and Mailly, of

10 Battalions, 10 Squadrons, and 4 Batteries.

The Regiment retires through St. Jure, in front of which some skirmishing occurs without the enemy making any more serious attack on that day.

He continued to occupy Longeville and the bridge in front of Les Menils. Numerous watchfires are burning behind Mailly.

The posts at Pouilly and Verny report in the evening that the enemy opposite to them is retiring on Marieulles, where watchfires become visible.

How does the Commander of the Reserve Division view his situation?

What does he intend to do

1. If the enemy early on the 4th May advances against Louvigny with the forces concentrated behind Raucourt?

2. If the Cavalry ascertains that the enemy still holds the height of Raucourt in order to secure his own communications, but has marched off with part of his troops by Sécourt against the railway?

3. If he should remain passive until the troops from Marieulles can debouch by Cheminot?

E

59TH PROBLEM. 1879.

Vide Plan 23 and Sketch Map 9.

An Eastern Corps has beaten the enemy on the right bank of the Fulda, and pushed him beyond Cassel on the 1st May. It determines to continue the pursuit during the following days in the direction of Arolsen with the Cavalry and the 21st Infantry Division.

22ND INFANTRY DIVISION:
44th Infantry Brig.   43rd Infantry Brig.
Regiment 94.   Regiment 95.

Regiment 32.   Regiment 83.

Uhlan Regiment 6.

2nd Division Field Artillery Regiment 27.
(24 guns.)
Engineer Company.

Divisional Pontoon Troop.

Ambulance Detachment.

To secure this advance against hostile forces, which are set in motion from Frankfurt-on-the-Main by Marburg, the 22nd Infantry Division is detached from Cassel to the left.

It reaches Holzhausen on the 2nd May, and pushes out Cavalry detachments towards the Ems.

In the evening trustworthy intelligence arrives that the enemy—about 20,000 strong—has arrived at Kerstenhausen, on the Frankfurt road.

What does the General of Division determine for the following day?

60TH PROBLEM. 1879.

Vide Plan 17 and Sketch Map 6.

The hostile Army having been repulsed beyond the Doubs, Belfort is to be besieged.

14TH ARMY CORPS.
28TH DIVISION:
56th Brigade.   55th Brigade.
22nd.   109th.

111th.   110th.

20th Dragoons.

1st Division Field Artillery Regiment 30.
(24 guns.)
2 Companies   Engineers.

Ambulance Detachment.

There is in the fortress, in addition to its normal war garrison, another mobile Brigade.

To observe the east front of the place the 1st Reserve Division has been pushed forward by Cernay* on Roppe and Pfaffans, the 2nd Reserve Division by Altkirch on Vezelois and Méroux. Under cover of detachments posted there,

* Sennheim.

29TH DIVISION:

58th Brigade.   57th Brigade.
   17th.   113th.
   ————   ————
   112th.   114th.
   ————   ————

21st Dragoons.
   ———

nd Division Field Artillery Regiment 30.
                (24 guns.)
1 Company ——— Engineers.

☒ Ambulance Detachment.

CORPS ARTILLERY:
Field Artillery Regiment 14.
        (48 guns.)

☒ Ambulance Detachment.

Trains.
————

and of their outposts, the troops are billeted in the villages as far back as the Madeleine and St. Nicolas brooks.

On the 1st June, the head of the 14th Army Corps, which is to complete the investment on the west bank of the Savoureuse, arrives at Sermamagny from the north, strength as per margin.

The close investment, at an average distance of 5,000 paces from the fortress, is to be completed by midday on the 3rd June.

Corps orders for the march of the 14th Army Corps on the 2nd June.

6IST PROBLEM. 1880.

Vide Plan 24.

The mobile 5th Infantry Division is on its march to the Rhine.

Regiment No. 35.   Regiment No. 48.
   ————   ————
Regiment No. 20.   Regiment No. 8.
   ————   ————
        Rifles No. 3.
           ————

Dragoon Regiment No. 12.
   ——— ——— ——— ———

st Division Field Artillery Regt. No. 18.
            (24 guns.)
—— 1st Company   ⎫
                       ⎬ of Engineer
☒ Divisional Pontoon   ⎬ Battalion
   Troop No. 1.   ⎭ No. 3.

☒ Ambulance Detachment No. 1.

☐ Field Hospital   ☐ Provision
   Nos. 1 and 2.   Column No. 1.

Having reached Paderborn on the 1st April it learns that behind Haaren a hostile Division has arrived, threatening the intended march to Gesecke on the 2nd.

The railway is destroyed.

How will the 5th Division arrange its march on the 2nd?

62ND PROBLEM.   1880.

Vide Plan 24.

The 5th Division, on the 2nd April, reached Gesecke, its Flank Detachment having been engaged.   A hostile party remained during the night near Drei Eichen ; large watchfires shine from the heights beyond the Alme.

The 60th Regiment has arrived at Gesecke from Erwitte as a reinforcement.   An attempt is to be made to defeat the enemy on the 3rd April.

How does the Commander of the Division intend to effect this ?

63RD PROBLEM.   1881.

Vide Plan 25.

Metz is threatened with siege.

In order to observe towards the west

3 Battalions, 1 Squadron, and 2 Sortie Batteries

are standing at Gravelotte.

Infantry Regiment No. 45.

1 Squadron Dragoons No. 9.

2 Batteries.

50 men from the Engineer Batt. No. 15.

They report the enemy advancing from Verdun.   His leading troops arrived at Vionville on the 1st July, and Cavalry patrols of the enemy were repulsed by dismounted Dragoons at Rezonville in the evening.

The fortress gets its full war garrison only on the 3rd July. The Governor charges the Detachment with preventing, as far as possible, the enemy from establishing himself on the plateau of Gravelotte until after the 2nd inst.

How will the Commander of the Detachment carry out his task ?

64TH PROBLEM. 1881.

Vide Plan 26 and Sketch Map 3.

The Army operating beyond the Oder, towards the east, has received intelligence that a hostile Corps is advancing in its rear from Stettin, on Berlin.

The 2nd Army Corps, with the 3rd Cavalry Brigade, has been sent back by Freienwalde for the protection of the capital.

Arrived at Werneuchen, it hears that the enemy had passed Bernau already in the forenoon. His strength was estimated at about 20,000 men.

The patrols pushing beyond Löhme were received with Infantry fire from the patches of wood near Helenenau.

A strong reconnoitring party advancing beyond Seefeld got into the cross-fire of Batteries stationed behind the Döring See, also behind the Pietzstall close to the high-road, and on the knolls south-east of the latter. On the open heights only isolated Infantry posts were seen, and west of Krummensee weak Cavalry Detachments gave way before ours.

2ND ARMY CORPS.

4TH INFANTRY DIVISION.   **3RD INFANTRY DIVISION.**

Infantry Regiments:

61.   49.   54.   34.

21.   9.   14.   2.

Rifle Battalion No. 2.

Hussar Regiment No. 5.   Dragoon Regiment No 3.

2nd Div. of Art. Regt. 17.   1st Div. of Art. Regt. 17.
(24 guns.)   (24 guns.)

2nd Engineer Company.   1st Engineer Company.

Divisional Pontoon Troop.   Divisional Pontoon Troop.

Ambulance Detach. No. 2.   Ambulance Detach. No. 1.

CORPS ARTILLERY:
Field Artillery Regiment No. 2.
H. A. Division.   2nd Division.   1st Division.
(54 guns.)

Ambulance Detachment No. 3.

Ammunition Columns and Trains.

3RD CAVALRY BRIGADE:
Uhlan Regiment No. 9.   Cuirassier Regiment No. 1.

It therefore appears that the hostile Corps is concentrated in a " position of readiness " at Blumberg.

The enemy being so close the Corps goes for the night into bivouac near Werneuchen.

Where is the enemy to be attacked to-morrow?

The answer to the question is not to be given in the shape of an order, but in that of a "memoir" on the situation and on the measures to be adopted.

65TH PROBLEM. 1882.

Vide Plan 27 and Sketch Map 8.

The 2nd Army Corps is marching from Neidenburg by Hohenstein to unite with the 1st Army Corps advancing on Wormditt.

FLANK DETACHMENT:

8th Infantry Brigade:
Infantry Regiment No. 21 ⎫
     ,,   ,,   61 ⎬ 7 Battalions.
Rifle Battalion   No. 2 ⎭
Dragoon Regiment No. 11, 4 Squadrons.
Field Artlly. Regt. No. 17, 2 Batteries.
1 Comp. Egr. Batt. No. 2, 1 Comp.

7 Battls., 4 Squads., 2 Batts., 1 Comp.

The former hears at Hohenstein that a hostile Eastern Corps is pushing towards Allenstein, and determines to make for the direction of Osterode. In order to secure its flank it sends off a right Flank Detachment, which after a long march on country roads reaches the neighbourhood of Langguth on the evening of April the 1st.

The Main Body on that day arrived at Osterode, and will, on the following day, under cover of the detachment, continue its march to Mohrungen. Its trains have been sent ahead under escort to Reussen.

The Flank Detachment is directed not to engage without need in any fight which would oblige the Main Body to interrupt its march in order to support it.

Only isolated Cavalry troops of the enemy reconnoitred towards the Passarge on the 1st of April, and they then retired to Alt-Schöneberg.

    1. What measures does the Commander of the Flank Detachment adopt for the night?

    2. How does he intend to solve his problem on the 2nd April?

66TH PROBLEM. 1882.

Vide Plan 27 and Sketch Map 8.

The enemy did not attack the lake defiles during the 2nd April and the Flank Detachment remained east of Horn. Dragoon patrols reconnoitring beyond Seubersdorf noticed numerous watchfires near Schlitt and Blankenberg, and found the enemy on the morning of the 3rd April engaged in constructing bridges across the Passarge above and below Deppen.

On that day the Flank Detachment moved forward early, by Willnau and Reichau, occupied the Ponarien Wood with Rifles, and took up a covered " position of readiness " behind the heights east of Herzogswalde.

The Main Body of the 2nd Corps starts from Mohrungen to Liebstadt, where its head arrives at 10 a.m. It intends to await, in a position between that place and the Passarge, the arrival of the 1st Corps, which will move from Wormditt by Kalkstein to Schwenkitten, but which cannot arrive there before the evening. Both Corps will then assume the offensive.

At 10 o'clock the enemy has crossed the Passarge and deployed astride of the road to Waltersdorf for attacking, as it appears, the 2nd Corps before the 1st joins.

The Commander of the Flank Detachment did not receive special instructions from the headquarters of the Corps.

How will he act in order to meet possible eventualities?

II.

SOLUTIONS AND CRITICISMS.

Sketch

for the Solution of the 1st Problem.

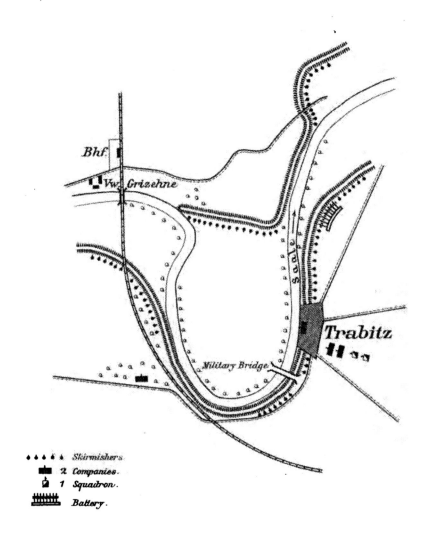

Bhf.

Vw. Grizehne

S. Saas

Trabitz

Military Bridge

♦ ♦ ♦ ♦ ♦   Skirmishers.

2 Companies.

1 Squadron.

Battery.

Scale $\frac{1}{25000}$.

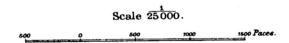

500   0   500   1000   1500 Paces.

Verlag d. Kgl. Hofbuchh. v. E. S. Mittler & Sohn, Berlin. (Kochstr. 68/70.)   Geogr. lith. Inst. u. Steindr. v. Wilhelm Greve, B

SOLUTION OF THE 1ST PROBLEM.

Vide accompanying sketch of the position of the Advanced Guard, after a hand sketch by General v. Moltke.

The passage of a river like the lower Saale by means of constructing a bridge cannot be effected opposite a watchful enemy either by day or night without his discovering and resisting it.

It must be forced.

The means to do so are the great strength of the attacking force, which can remain concentrated while the defender must divide and the greater effect of the 12-pr. Battery. It is only a question of making that superiority felt at the proper point.

As soon as this principle is realized there is only the choice left between Dröbel and Trabitz. At both places the passage can be forced in the face of the enemy.

Against the former there is the difficulty of advancing further beyond the steep slopes of the valley and across the Bode behind which section of the ground the Battalion from Bernburg will join its Main Body from Calbe.

At Trabitz we encounter at once the main force of the enemy, yet he is not able to prevent a crossing, and still less to prohibit the further debouching of the united Southern Detachment.

According to my opinion, Trabitz is therefore to be chosen, 12 miles from Cöthen in the most direct line to Magdeburg.

That point is reached with ease about midday.

The passage will be effected in 2 to 3 hours, after which the attack upon the enemy takes place with united forces.

Since he does not find any tenable section of the ground, is much weaker than we, and is threatened on his line of retreat, he will only be able to try to gain so much time as is necessary to draw in his Battalion from Bernburg.

SOLUTION OF THE 2ND PROBLEM.

The reconnaissance of yesterday showed that the enemy is standing behind the Prüm in a strong but somewhat extended position considering the number of his troops.

Besides the detachments which he has shown, he will probably have one Battalion in the Tetenbusch, and one in the town of Prüm ; his reserve, therefore, only about 4 Battalions, 6 Squadrons, and 2 Batteries, is to be looked for behind the Calvarien Berg as the only point from which he can support both wings and secure the defile of Niedermehlen, so important for his retreat.

The ground makes the left wing of the enemy and his front almost unassailable ; the right wing is weaker, where the crest on our side of the valley commands it. Nieder-Prüm cannot be maintained by the enemy. Niedermehlen can be reached from there by a shorter road than from Dausfeld or Hermespand.

An attack on the enemy's right wing bars his roads by Schönecken and Lünebach, on which he can effect a junction with the Western Army, and threatens his retreat by Sellerich and Malmedy.

This attack would also endanger our own communications, if such could not be transferred to the Schönecken road, on account of the advance of the Eastern Army towards Trier.

The dispositions for attack would have to be based on these circumstances.

Advanced Guard: 2 Battalions, 1 Troop of Cavalry, and 1 Howitzer Battery.

Rendezvous at 5 o'clock west of Büdesheim. Advances by the Prüm road, forms for attack on the other side of the Nims, moves to the height east of Prüm. The Advanced Guard has to prevent an advance of the enemy, to detain his left wing in the Tetenbusch and the town, and immediately pushes home the attack, if the enemy withdraws from there.

Main Body: 6 Battalions, 2 Squadrons, 2 12-pr. and 1 6-pr. Batteries.

Rendezvous south-west of Büdesheim. Marches in two columns, each with a weak Infantry Advanced Guard close in front, by Fleringen and Wallersheim respectively, on Rommersheim. The columns form for attack west and south respectively of the latter place.

The two 12-pr. Batteries with one Battalion form up on the heights south-west of Held—all the rest moving through the Ellwerath gorge—against Nieder-Prüm, from which place the enemy, if he has occupied it, is to be dislodged. Then the 6-pr. Battery on the low height south of that place. Cavalry in rear.

Reserve: 4 Battalions, 9¾ Squadrons, and two Batteries.

Rendezvous south-west of Büdesheim. Follows for the present the Main Body in two columns and halts under cover behind the height west of Rommersheim until the attack on Nieder-Prüm is decided. Then again follows the Main Body, *i.e.,* the Infantry and Field Batteries by Nieder-Prüm, while the Cavalry and Horse Artillery Battery try to get over the Prüm at an accelerated pace lower down by Ellwerath.

If the Main Body has succeeded in debouching from Nieder-Prüm the 12-pr. Batteries will follow and join the reserve.

If the Advanced Guard cannot penetrate at Prüm it takes up a position at Held, and occupies Nieder-Prüm.

An attack with 10 Battalions, 12 Squadrons, and 5 Batteries on the Calvarien Berg is intended, the Cavalry on the left wing.

Reports to the General commanding are to be sent to the height east of Nieder-Prüm, where the 12-pr. Battery is posted.

The Trains are ordered from Gerolstein to Balesfeld.

SOLUTION OF THE 3RD PROBLEM.

The hilly country between Driburg and Paderborn presents different sections, which are particularly suitable for defensive occupation and do not leave to the enemy full freedom for offensive movements.

For the present purpose, however, only the two sections, Bucke-Schwanei and the heights north and south of the Brocks Berg should be considered. A position further in advance in the direction of Driburg would have to be dismissed unconditionally on account of the strongly wooded Egge highlands in rear ; one further back, *i.e.,* between Paderborn and Brocks Berg, from the mere fact that these positions are situated in front.

If we compare now the above-mentioned positions with each other, that north and south of the Brocks Berg is the better one as a defensive position. An envelopment in the north seems out of the question considering the mountainous character of the country, and an attack can only take place on the high-road from Driburg. Nevertheless, I do not think it suitable for our use, because the enemy will not force that position. He will sweep round on Herbran and Dörenhagen, and thus succeed in obliging the Corps to retire on Dahl and Harter Grund without firing a single shot.

The enemy, if attacked in flank, can go behind the Jageser Wasser. The range of heights from Bucke to Schwanei with the railway embankment in front may be therefore considered as the main position. On the eastern side the enemy steps from the wood on to the railway embankment, and from there he is obliged to climb the sharply rising heights on open ground. On the north the position is bounded by the very hilly ground of Altenbecken, on the south by the swampy ground beginning at the Gefe Bruch. The enemy is obliged to attack this position, if we mean at all to occupy one between Driburg and Paderborn. It will then be mainly a question of the terrain from Bucke to the point where the railway crosses the road from Schwanei to Neuenherse extending not quite 3½ miles. The enemy's attacking force in that case can either select the high-road from Driburg or the road Dringenberg—Neuenherse—Schwanei and the intermediate communications, or, what is the most likely, several of these lines at the same time. But he must in any case attack the position Bucke-Schwanei. These places are only 4,000 paces apart, they command the exits from the wood across the railway embankment, their line of retreat leads by the high-road to Paderborn, and the junction of the high-road with the road from Schwanei is a position for the reserve as if meant for such by nature, being admirably favoured by the ground. Whether the village of Bucke itself is to be occupied for obstinate defence or whether the crucial point of the position is not rather to be shifted to Schwanei with the Lim Berg as Artillery position cannot be determined by the map, since it will chiefly depend on the position of the railway in relation to the ground.

The Advanced Guard must occupy with pickets and sentries the line, Stell Berg—Iburg—Trappisten Kloster and the Nethen Berg, and select as lines of retreat the high road to Bucke, the road from Koch to Schwanei and from Neuenherse to Schwanei.

The Main Body of the Advanced Guard will be best posted at Koch, south of the Haus Heide, and from there be able to meet an advance of the enemy in all directions.

If the enemy should advance in several columns, the Advanced Guard will have to split accordingly, and be eventually supported by the Main Body.

The heights at Lackenicht, at the Haus Heide, and the railway embankment at the junction of the road to Schwanei are positions for the reserves of the Advanced Guard.

SOLUTION OF THE 4TH PROBLEM.

To the General 1st Division,

„ „ 2nd Division,

„ „ 1st Cavalry Division,

„ „ commanding Advanced Guard.

The pursuit to-morrow is to be continued with the utmost vigour.

For this purpose the Army Corps will be echeloned between Passendorf and Schlettau in such a way that the enemy will be thrown by superior forces into the defile of Halle, but at the same time a crossing to the right bank of the Saale be effected.

. The three Cavalry Regiments and the Horse Artillery Battery with which the Advanced Guard was reinforced will to-night rejoin the Cavalry Division, to which also the two Horse Artillery Batteries of the Reserve Artillery will be handed over.

The Pontoon Train and Engineer Detachment will be for to-morrow attached to the 2nd Infantry Brigade.

All the troops concentrated at Langenbogen will rendezvous to-morrow morning at four o'clock in front of the bivouac, ready to start.

The Cavalry Regiment of the 2nd Division and the 4th Infantry Brigade direct their course by Bennstedt on Zscherben, the 3rd Infantry Brigade by Eisdorf, and to the south round Zscherben.

Both Brigades form up beyond that village. The Division moves at daybreak into the alignment Angersdorf—Königliche Braunkohlen Grube (on the map " Kön. Brkgr.").

The Divisional Cavalry *in front* of the left wing of the 3rd Brigade.

The 2nd Infantry Brigade, with the Pontoon Train (at the head, under escort), marches by Mittel Deutschenthal—Grosse Rüster to Schlettau. The construction of the bridges will begin at once at Rohrlagge, the spot previously reconnoitered. The Brigade is to employ the necessary Infantry and Artillery to carry it out.

The Reserve Artillery will follow the 2nd Infantry Brigade.

The Cavalry Division will march by Ober Deutschenthal in the direction of Beuchlitzer Weinberg, and form up in a covered position in the valley of Sauerbreite.

The Advanced Guard covers the deployment of the 2nd Division concentrates before daybreak against Pfaffendorf, briskly attacks this village from the west side, and is to be supported by the 3rd Brigade from the south. Nietleben will be observed by the Cavalry (two Regiments). As soon as the enemy gives way he is to be vigorously pursued.

I await full reports on the course of this fight at the Angersdorf Galgen Berg.

As soon as the bridges are passable the 2nd Infantry Brigade crosses and moves up as far as the height of Wörmlitz and occupies the village, the Batteries on the right wing towards Röpzig Zgl. (Ziegelei).

It is immediately followed by the Cavalry Division, still consisting of 20 Squadrons and 24 guns Horse Artillery, after deducting a Regiment sent to Merseburg. The Division at once detaches a force on Ammendorf in order to prevent a crossing of the Elster by hostile Cavalry from Merseburg. Should the enemy already be retreating on Leipzig he is to be attacked without delay.

The further passage of the 4th, 3rd, and eventually of the Advanced Guard Brigades over the Pontoon bridge I shall order according to circumstances on the spot.

The Ammunition Columns and Field Hospitals are directed to Beuchlitz, the Provision Columns remain under their present escort behind the Salza at Langenbogen.

Bivouac, Langenbogen, date . . . .

SOLUTION OF THE 5TH PROBLEM.

Missing.

SOLUTION OF THE 6TH PROBLEM.

DISPOSITION FOR THE 13TH MARCH.

Headquarters, Frankfurt-on-the-Oder,
Evening, 12th March.

The Eastern Corps moved to-night into Drossen, a Division occupying a position at Kunersdorf. That Division will be attacked without delay to-morrow forenoon.

The 1st Division has to detain the enemy in front at Kunersdorf, the 4th Brigade attacks him on the left flank. The 3rd Brigade opens the passage through the wood for the Cavalry, and secures its debouching into the plain of Zohlow.

For this purpose the 1st Division forms up behind the Laudons Grund* and advances at 9.30 against Kunersdorf.

The Reserve Artillery will get its orders from the 1st Division, to the movements of which it will conform.

The 4th Infantry Brigade starts at 8 o'clock from the Chaussee-haus near the Juden Kirchhof by the Crossen road ; 1,000 paces from Chausseehaus it inclines to the left, turns the chain of lakes and swamps extending down to Kunersdorf, and at once advances to attack the enemy's left wing through the Frankfurter Forst.

The 3rd Brigade divides into two columns.

The 3rd Infantry Regiment and the Battery immediately follow the 4th Brigade on the high-road through the Schwetiger Revier, and then march without stopping from behind that Brigade by the straight ride leading to the farm of Scheibler.†

The 3rd Landwehr Regiment and the Divisional Cavalry march at 8 o'clock by Grund Schäferei along the rides of the Schwetiger Revier, then follow the boundary path between Frankfurter and Neuendorfer Forst ‡ on Sorge.

The 3rd Brigade occupies the Schweden-Damm, Sorge, and the little wood on the Birken See.

The Cavalry Division, strengthened by two Horse Artillery Batteries of the Reserve, follows immediately behind the 3rd Infantry Brigade, the 2nd Cavalry Brigade behind the 3rd Infantry Regiment, the 1st Cavalry Brigade behind the 3rd Landwehr Regiment. The Division tries to reach as soon as possible the open plain of Zohlow.

---

* Junction of the high-road to Kunersdorf and the road to Trettin.   † On the Scheibler See.
‡ Küniglich Reppensche Forst.

F

The General commanding will be with the 4th Infantry Brigade and then go to Sorge, whence the further movements will be regulated.

ADDITIONAL TO THE 1ST DIVISION:

The detachments of the 1st Division left behind in the entrenchments will be drawn in as soon as it crosses the section of the ground of Kunersdorf.

VERBALLY TO THE COMMISSARIAT:

All vehicles remain till further orders on the left bank of the Oder ; only a light Field Hospital follows about noon by the Drossen road as far as the Hühner Fliess.

TO THE COMMANDER OF ARTILLERY:

1 Ammunition Column in the same direction.

SOLUTION OF THE 7TH PROBLEM.

The ground between Drossen and Kunersdorf, after this point is lost, nowhere affords to the Eastern Corps a favourable battlefield. The enemy is superior in numbers. A near and broad base allows him the greatest freedom of movement.

All these disadvantages can only be compensated for if the Corps again approaches Posen.

It will therefore not seek battle to-day, but as soon as possible begin an orderly retreat.

But previously to this the 1st Division must necessarily be picked up, and if this cannot be done a battle must be risked for that purpose.

The enemy has marched with his Infantry 9 miles, with his Cavalry and Artillery 13½ miles ; he had two to three Brigades in action ; about noon he has not yet debouched from the wood. It is therefore not probable that he can bring on anything decisive to-day. But it is possible, and one must be fully prepared for action.

The Eastern Corps, under these circumstances, has the no small advantage of having together two intact Divisions, while the enemy must necessarily advance through the wood in separate columns. If the Eastern Corps splits its forces as well, it loses the only advantage it has.

The Corps, therefore, must stand ready for action and concentrated.

If the enemy advances by many roads he will debouch on a front so much more extended ; if he uses only few roads his columns will have so much greater depth. In the first case he needs time for uniting, in the latter for deploying his columns.

But it is just a question of gaining time.

If the 1st Division has broken off the action at the right time, it is able to retreat by the Drossen road, and the junction is effected without difficulty. If, on the other hand, it is forced away on Bischofsee, it needs one to two hours in order to effect its junction with the Main Body, and this time *must* be procured for it.

Upon this the following measures are based :

The Advanced Guard * continues to advance on the Kunersdorf road, but gets the order to halt at the Schweden-Damm and to occupy the bridge there and at Scheibler.

The Detachment of the 1st Division stands at Sorge.

Both, the Advanced Guard and this Detachment, are hastily reinforced each by ½ a Battery of Horse Artillery under escort of 2 Squadrons each.

The object is not so much to prevent his debouching as to render it difficult, to delay it, and to find out where the enemy is coming with his main force.

If the enemy's turning movement should make a wider sweep to the right, it is just what we could desire.

All the rest of the Corps, 9 Battalions, 20 Squadrons, and 6 Batteries, will stand in rendezvous position at Kobert.

The 1st Division, wherever it may have crossed the Fliess, will get the order to retire on Zohlow. Part of the Cavalry Division is available if it should require direct support.

Retreat will commence as soon as the 1st Division approaches Zohlow.

All three Divisions† unite at Zohlow.

The Rear Guard will be composed of the 4th Infantry Brigade, the whole Cavalry Division, and three Batteries Horse Artillery. It follows the Main Body at first at Artillery range. All are marching in complete battle order.

Columns of route can be formed only after the enemy's pressure ceases.

* Assumed as 3 Battalions, 4 Squadrons, and 2 Batteries.
† *Viz.*, the two Infantry Divisions and the Cavalry Division.

SOLUTION OF THE 8TH PROBLEM.

At Glatz, at Silberberg, in order to be able to oppose in time a debouching at Braunau as well as at Nachod and Reinerz. It would be better further in advance, but then there is no possibility of doing justice in both directions.

SOLUTION OF THE 9TH PROBLEM.
Missing.

SOLUTION OF THE 10TH PROBLEM.
Missing.

SOLUTION OF THE 11TH PROBLEM.

The Division is ordered to cover Berlin. The enemy's columns are still separated, and singly weaker than the Division. Since both columns advance separately, the Division cannot bar the road to Berlin by occupying the Tasdorf defile, and is, on the other hand, too weak for extending as far as Erkner.

It has therefore nothing else left but to hinder the junction of the hostile columns, and, in order to gain that object, to beat them singly. But this again is only possible by an offensive stroke. It would therefore seem the most correct to advance beyond the Tasdorf defile and to oppose the hostile forces, which are advancing from Müncheberg and necessarily obliged to move on to Tasdorf. The Division will therefore, on the 2nd June, be stationed near Herzfelde, and attack the enemy after his debouching from the defile of Heidekrug.

The Tasdorf defile remains occupied in order that we may eventually withdraw again behind it.

SOLUTION OF THE 12TH PROBLEM.

The Division will be withdrawn for the night behind the defile at Tasdorf, and will bivouac in the district between Tasdorf and Vogelsdorf somewhere north of Grünelinde.

The Advanced Guard takes post at Herzfelde, but keeps in touch with the enemy. The defile at Erkner will be occupied by one

Battalion and two troops of Cavalry; this Detachment also observes the defile at Woltersdorf.

The movements on the 3rd June will depend on the enemy's operations. The Division will oppose his debouching from the Tasdorf defile. The Advanced Guard keeps in touch with the enemy, and, if pressed by him, retires on Tasdorf.

SOLUTION OF THE 13TH PROBLEM.

It is apparent from the enemy's enterprises on the 3rd June that he feels too weak for attacking the Tasdorf defile in front. But it cannot yet be discerned from his movements in what manner he intends to operate further. From the intelligence about the arrival of a Battalion at Wrietzen it may be concluded that reinforcements are expected from there, and that next it is intended to unite with these; it is also possible that the Eastern Corps itself has detached a Battalion there in order to gain a fresh line of retreat.

Now, if the enemy will not advance on Tasdorf, his next line of operation is by Straussberg or Wilkendorf—Gielsdorf to Alt Landsberg, if he does not take the still longer detour Prötzel—Werneuchen.

But as the defile at Straussberg, as well as that of Tasdorf, is a very important obstacle, it remains very questionable what the enemy will do.

Since the Division (in all now 15 Battalions, 8 Squadrons, and 4 Batteries) is ordered to cover Berlin, and from its position at Tasdorf can advance everywhere, while, on the other hand, a useless marching to and fro as long as the hostile movements do not allow us to recognize a distinct intention, would only prematurely absorb the strength of the troops, it appears the most practical to leave the Division in its position at Grünelinde. To this end the Battalion should be drawn in from Erkner, but a Regiment of Infantry, 3 Squadrons, and 2 guns should be detached to Straussberg. The Advanced Guard, with a strength of 2 Battalions, 2 Squadrons, and 2 guns, occupies a position at Zinndorf. The Cavalry must keep in touch with the enemy.

SOLUTION OF THE 14TH PROBLEM.
Missing.

SOLUTION OF THE 15TH PROBLEM.
Missing.

SOLUTION OF THE 16TH PROBLEM.
Missing.

SOLUTION OF THE 17TH PROBLEM.

Measures of the Southern Division for the 2nd June :

1. The Advanced Guard (3 Battalions, 1 Squadron, and 1 Battery) will be reinforced by a Battery from the Main Body, and has to maintain Weissenfels against any attack.

2. The Main Body of the Division remains on the 2nd June at Dippelsdorf.

3. It is to be ascertained by reconnaissance whether the Main Body of the enemy is following its advanced Division, which is in bivouac with its Main Body behind and between Markwerben and Burgwerben, or moving towards another point of the Saale. Two Detachments are sent out for this purpose :

   (a) The 3rd Infantry Regiment,

      2 Companies Rifles,

      1 Detachment Engineers,

      6 Squadrons (3 Squadrons Uhlans and 3 Squadrons Hussars),

      4 guns Horse Artillery,

         move across the Saale by Plotha and the railway bridge above Eulau at 5 a.m. on the 2nd June. From there a Battalion is to be detached to the Saale bridge north of Naumburg, reconnoitring to Freiburg. The rest of the Infantry, the Rifles, and two guns occupy Goseck and the wood south of Dobichau. The Cavalry with two Horse Artillery guns advance by Marckröhlitz. Individual officers with well-mounted orderlies are to be sent forward as far as possible.

   (b) 1 Company Rifles
      1 Detachment Engineers } On wagons.

1 Squadron Hussars,
2 guns Horse Artillery,
 will march to Dürrenberg at 3 a.m. on the 2nd
June. The Rifles occupy Fährendorf. The
Squadron on Rossbach and as far as Merseburg.
The two guns are only eventually taken over
the bridge ; the Engineers prepare the bridge for
demolition.

Both Detachments remain in their positions until further orders.

The rapid transmission of reports is to be ensured by Cavalry relays, the positions of which are to be reported here.

SOLUTION OF THE 18TH PROBLEM.

Dippelsdorf, 6 p.m.

1. As learned from the reconnaissance, the enemy's Main Army had, up to this hour, not yet advanced as far as the Saale. I expect, therefore, to be able to advance to-morrow, the 3rd June, in the early morning, unmolested by it on the left bank of the Saale by Eulau, so as to force the Northern Division to give up its position at Markwerben by threatening its right flank or by an attack on its right wing.

2. I perceive therein the most suitable means for enabling the Southern Army to debouch from Weissenfels, and have therefore already ordered the reconnoitring troops on the other side of the river to remain west of Goseck, under cover of the strongly occupied patches of wood, and their Main Body with the Cavalry to bivouac near Eulau ; both bridges will be specially guarded.

The Advanced Guard will remain at Weissenfels, and I request that a Rifled Battery be sent there to-day, which to-morrow morning from Beutitz, supported by the 12-pr. Battery near Trompete, will force the enemy's Batteries east of Markwerben to limber up, or will silence them. Only when this is done are two Battalions of the Advanced Guard to cross the bridges ; one will remain in occupation of the town. All the rest of the Division will march to-morrow at 4 a.m. to the Eulau bridge, form up on the other side west of the village of Eulau, and then advance, 10 Battalions, 7 Squadrons, and 3½ Batteries strong, in the direction of Marckröhlitz. The Cavalry on the left wing will reconnoitre the ground on the left flank, to the greatest distance possible. All further measures will be adopted on the spot in proportion to the enemy's resistance.

The advance against Marckröhlitz cannot take place before 9 o'clock, but will be carried out by 10 o'clock at the latest, conformably to which the advance of the Army from the Rippach to the Saale is to be timed.

The effect of my attack on the behaviour of the enemy at Marckröhlitz will be perfectly visible from the heights of Weissenfels, and the Army will begin to debouch in accordance therewith.

SOLUTION OF THE 19TH PROBLEM.

The measures of the Northern Division will have to be such as cause delay, since it is not a question of preventing the passage of the hostile Army, but rather of permitting it, and of temporizing the action only long enough for our own Army to take up the intended position, in such a manner, however, that our movements are screened.

In order to attain that object the Division will hold the line, Marckröhlitz—Obschütz.

Against bodies debouching from Weissenfels, there remain in position:

> 2 Battalions,
> 2 Squadrons,
> 1 Battery Horse Artillery.

The Infantry occupies Markwerben. The Horse Artillery Battery, under escort of both Squadrons, keeps the bridge under fire; against superior Artillery it will draw in towards Markwerben.

If Markwerben is forced, the Detachment retires slowly on Storkau—Obschütz.

For opposing the passage over the Eulau bridge,

> 3 Battalions,
> 2 Squadrons,
> 1 Battery

are detached to Marckröhlitz. Marckröhlitz will be occupied by one Battalion; the rest remains behind that village as a reserve. Marckröhlitz is to be obstinately defended. One Battalion remains advanced towards Uechteritz, and will retire on the Main Body if Markwerben is given up.

> The Main Body: 9 Battalions,
> 4 Squadrons,
> 2 Batteries

takes up a position hidden in the Brosig Grund; in case of the enemy advancing from Guseck on Uechteritz, it will strike against his flank.

At sunrise to-morrow, about 4 o'clock, the Division will have taken up the positions referred to.

Reports will find the Commander on the Donners Berg, north of the Brosig Grund.

SOLUTION OF THE 20TH PROBLEM.

From the course of the action it may be concluded that the Southern Army will not cross the Saale in the face of the enemy and accept a battle with the Saale defiles in its rear. It has secured the defiles in order to be able to assume the offensive at any moment, as soon as the Northern Army withdraws.

By its position on the Rippach, it seems inclined to defend the Saale line from Naumburg, downwards, as far as the Dürrenberg railway bridge, and, in consequence of its possession of the defiles, is in a position to watch the movements of the Northern Army.

SOLUTION OF THE 21ST PROBLEM.
Missing.

SOLUTION OF THE 22ND PROBLEM.
Missing.

SOLUTION OF THE 23RD PROBLEM.
Missing.

SOLUTION OF THE 24TH PROBLEM.
Missing.

SOLUTION OF THE 25TH PROBLEM.

The Commander of the Detachment determines not to hold Hermeskeil, but rather to retire slowly and to make for the road to Malborn, in order to be able to observe the road by Birkenfeld. He intends to retire only so far as the hostile Detachment follows, so as not to lose touch of it.

SOLUTION OF THE 26TH PROBLEM.

The Main Body will bivouac in the valley of the Thalfanger Bach, at the northern exit of Thronecken. The outposts (2 Companies and ½ Squadron) have to cover the section Geisfeld—Malborn— road from Thronecken, on the Malborn brook, on both flanks. Cavalry patrols are to be pushed out on the following morning by the roads Thalfang—Birkenfeld and Trier—Hermeskeil.

If the enemy attacks on the 3rd April, the Detachment will withdraw on Thalfang—Morbach, should that road be still free; otherwise the Detachment will give way on Berg, subsequently taking the direction of Mülheim. If the enemy does not follow, the Detachment will remain until the patrols, sent by the road Trier—Hermeskeil, bring definite information; the Advanced Guard (2 Companies and ½ Squadron) moves again towards the Thiergarten settlement, in order not to lose touch.

SOLUTION OF THE 27TH PROBLEM.

From the movements of the enemy, it can be gathered that he has not chosen the direction of Trier, but of Berncastel—Trarbach. Whether he is marching in two columns by the roads Nohfelden— Birkenfeld and Wadern—Hermeskeil, or whether a strong Detachment is marching only by the latter as a Flank Guard, cannot be determined with certainty. From what the prisoners and country folks say it is not quite clear whether it is the Main Body of the Corps which is announced to arrive at Birkenfeld, or whether it is not rather its Advanced Guard only. As the Corps became available at Saarlouis on the 1st April, and can thus arrive at Birkenfeld on the 3rd, the distance being only two marches, it is, in any case, to be assumed that the enemy has arrived with his available forces about as far as Birkenfeld.

On the further advance of the enemy the Detachment will therefore retire on Berncastel, first gaining the road Morbach—Berncastel, and then continuing observations. It will at once detach a force to Berncastel in order to keep open its retreat by this point.

SOLUTION OF THE 28TH PROBLEM.

The 16th Division can still very well arrive at Berncastel for the defence of the Lower Mosel. At midday on the 3rd April it receives the intelligence referred to, and has therefore the 4th and 5th April still available, since the enemy cannot reach the Mosel with his leading troops before the 5th April, and thus cannot force it until the 6th.

To cross the Mosel would not appear suitable, as retreat is endangered by the superiority of the enemy and as the Division can much more successfully oppose his passage; neither does a direct defence of the Mosel seem to answer the purpose, since the point of crossing remains doubtful and the attempt at defence would only result in a frittering away of the forces.

If the Division keeps concentrated at Platten, occupying the bridges at Berncastel and Mülheim, it is in a position to make a timely advance in every direction and to fall upon the flank of anything debouching from Berncastel or Mülheim.

SOLUTION OF THE 29TH PROBLEM.

From the reports of the advanced Detachments we may conclude that, on the day of arrival of the Division on the 1st June, the 3,000 men from Potsdam have arrived at Brandenburg.

This body seems to be pushed forward as an Advanced Guard in order to secure Brandenburg with its bridge at Plaue.

The Eastern Division, following behind, will therefore base itself on Brandenburg. On the 1st June, in the evening, it is still at Berlin; it will not march therefore until the 2nd June to Potsdam, and from there advance on the 3rd. It will probably not use the highroad to Brandenburg, as the ground adjoining the high-road is not passable, and as the straight line from Potsdam to Magdeburg leads by Lehnin—Ziesar. It will therefore on the 3rd June push by Lehnin on Golzow and on the following day move towards the high-road which leads from Ziesar to Möckern. At Ziesar it will unite with the Advanced Guard sent ahead to keep open its line of retreat by Grüningen on Brandenburg. A small detachment at Plaue suffices for the defence of the bridge there; the Division is therefore secure on that flank.

If the Eastern Division has reached Ziesar and united with the Advanced Guard it is 15,000 to 16,000 strong, superior to our Division,

well based, and has got over the most difficult part of the ground.
From that moment the Western Division will hardly still be able to
prevent a further advance of the Eastern Division.

Thus, the mode of action for the Western Division is apparent.
It must prevent a junction of the Advanced Guard with the Eastern
Division. As it need not yet anticipate a collision with the Eastern Divi-
sion, on the following day (2nd June), it must attack the Advanced
Guard at Brandenburg, take possession of Brandenburg, and thus
delay a junction of the Advanced Guard with its Division.

SOLUTION OF THE 30TH PROBLEM.

The Western Division which is to cover the investment of Magdeburg will oppose the advance of the Eastern Division everywhere,
wherever it may happen to be. The operations of the Eastern Division must therefore be directed towards reaching Magdeburg by the
shortest road, and accepting battle wherever offered. An advance by
the high-road from Potsdam to Magdeburg is out of the question, as the ground does not permit movements astride the high-
road or of the railway embankment, and the enemy, in possession of
Brandenburg, can successfully oppose any attack. The Division must
therefore choose the only remaining and shortest line, Lehnin—
Golzow—Ziesar. There are in this direction two large sections of
the ground at Lehnin and Golzow ; the latter especially is of particular importance, as the soft meadows and the swampy ground allow
an advance on only a few roads. There are no points of crossing at
all except at Reckahn—Golzow—Cammer, if the Division will not turn
still further south as far as Brück, whereby, however, it would entirely
give up the connection with its Advanced Guard.

It remains now questionable whether the enemy will not, after
all, resist at the first section, namely, that of Lehnin.

This, it is true, may be assumed from his bivouac fires at Rotscherlinde, as he would otherwise probably have already retired behind
the second obstacle. The Eastern Division can wish for nothing
better than to succeed in bringing about an action there.

If it succeeds in pushing the enemy away on Brandenburg he
loses his line of retreat, and can no longer hinder the Division in its
further advance.

It is difficult to force Lehnin itself, and in the north there is only

Nahmitz, where an advance could be made ; but this would draw the enemy off from Brandenburg. No other course is therefore left but to turn the position from the south.

DISPOSITION.

The Division will continue its march to-morrow on Magdeburg and take the direction Baumgartenbrück—Petzow—Bliesendorf—Lehnin—Michelsdorf. It is probable that the Division will be engaged in an action, and the troops have therefore to march prepared for that before reaching Petzow.

The Division will start in two columns.

The right column, consisting of 6 Battalions, 2 Squadrons, and 2 Batteries, follows the direction above ordered as far as Bliesendorf, preceded by a special Advanced Guard. If Lehnin is occupied it takes the direction of Schwiena—Rädel, where it will fight a temporising action, until the left column begins to act.

The left column, 4 Battalions, 4 Squadrons, and 1½ Batteries, will march from Petzow on Claistow, turn the Luch near Canin in a southerly direction, and march to Busendorf. Thence it moves on Tornow farm, leaving Rädel to the north.

As soon as the left column has arrived, the right column moves on Michelsdorf, while the former marches on Oberjünne, envelops the enemy's right wing, and tries to act upon the rear of the position. The cavalry will find opportunity for action in the clearings of the wood. Towards Golzow must be observed.

The left column starts at 6 a.m., the right column follows at 7. The Commander will accompany the Advanced Guard of the right column.

SOLUTION OF THE 31ST PROBLEM.

The position of the defile of Lehnin has its weakness on the right flank and in rear ; especially any retreat is dangerous, because it must go through the difficult defile of Reckahn—Golzow.

ADVANCED GUARD :

1st Regiment.

Hussar Regiment.

1st Battery.

MAIN BODY :

3rd Regiment.

2 Battalions 4th Regiment.

1¾ Squadron Dragoons.

2nd Battery.

RESERVE DETACHMENT IN GOLZOW :

2 Battalions 2nd Regiment.

1 Troop Dragoons.

½ 3rd Battery.

DETACHMENT BEFORE BRANDENBURG :

1 Battn. 2nd Regt.   1 Battn. 4th Regt.

2 Squadrons Dragoons.

½ 3rd Battery.

If, however, battle is to be accepted there, it will not be confined to the defence of the defiles of Lehnin, but the main issue will rather have to be shifted to the debouchment of the enemy from the wood between Rädel and Oberjünne. The enemy cannot frontally force the section Nahmitz—Lehnin—Schwiena—Rädel ; few troops will suffice to prevent any advance.

The enemy is therefore obliged to make a turning movement, and this he can execute only between Rädel and Oberjünne.

It appears, therefore, the most practical course to concentrate the main forces west of Michelsdorf in order to be able to deal blows in all directions. At the same time, however, Golzow must be strongly occupied in order to secure the line of retreat and to threaten any advance by Oberjünne.

The passage of the Havel will be prevented, or at least made seriously difficult to the hostile Advanced Guard, which is in Brandenburg, by a few troops, as it can execute it only in face of the enemy.

To this end the following should therefore be ordered :

The Division will oppose to-morrow, the 3rd June, the advance of the enemy from Potsdam, and accept battle in the neighbourhood of Lehnin.

The Advanced Guard starts at 5 a.m., and moves into the position Nahmitz — Lehnin — Schwiena— Rädel ; the Cavalry goes towards Bliesendorf, and as far as the neighbourhood of Petzow.

The Main Body and the Reserve Detachment cook in Golzow

and have to arrange so that at 10 a.m. the former is concentrated in a position west of Michelsdorf (the Battery on the Windmill height east of the place, the two Squadrons behind it), the latter in Golzow.

The outposts, as before, remain in their position at Brandenburg, and have to observe as far as Plaue. If, after all, the enemy effects a crossing, they will retire eventually on Göttin and Reckahn.

I shall be on the height west of the Gohlitz See.

All carriages are to be directed by Golzow on Ziesar.

SOLUTION OF THE 32ND PROBLEM.

DISPOSITION OF THE SOUTHERN CORPS FOR THE 2ND JUNE.

Zossen, 1st June, 1866, 6 p.m.

The Corps will continue its advance to-morrow on Berlin, and attack the enemy wherever he makes a stand.

His Rear Guard is to be drawn into a vigorous action in order to oblige the enemy to come to the rescue with larger forces. For this purpose the Advanced Guard will to-morrow be strengthened by the 2nd Cavalry Regiment and the Howitzer Battery, which are to be sent from the Reserve so as to reach Gross Machnow at 5.45.

The Advanced Guard, 3 Battalions, 6 Squadrons, and 2 Batteries, starts at 6 a.m. from Gross Machnow, and Mittenwalde respectively, and marches on Klein Kienitz.

The Main Body marches in two columns, viz. :

Left column, the Reserve : 6 Battalions, 8 Squadrons, and 2 Batteries from Zossen, by Gross Machnow, on Dahlewitz. Time of starting from Zossen, 4 a.m.

Right column, the Main Body : 6 Battalions, 2 Squadrons, and 2 Batteries, by Mittenwalde and Gross Kienitz. Time of starting from Mittenwalde, 5 a.m.

Both columns will therefore march abreast beyond Machnow and Mittenwalde.

Should the enemy defend the bog section at Kienitz, the left column continues marching to Dahlewitz without stopping, and attacks from there. If the enemy tries to maintain himself behind the section of Glasow, I shall issue the orders for the attack from the Gross Kienitz hill.

If the enemy still further persists in retreating without interruption, the Advanced Guard will continue its pursuit as far as its strength will permit. It will be supported therein by the Reserve Cavalry.

Both columns, so far as they are not immediately covered by the Advanced Guard, have to reconnoitre in front and on the flanks with their Cavalry, particularly beyond the Glasow section, the left column on its left flank.

The Trains, leaving the high-road clear, remain east of Zossen until orders arrive to advance.

The Commander will march with the right column.

SOLUTION OF THE 33RD PROBLEM.

DISPOSITION OF THE NORTHERN DIVISION FOR THE 2ND JUNE.

Glasow, 1st June, 6 p.m.

The Division, early to-morrow, takes up a covered rendezvous position behind the patches of wood between Mahlow and Blankenfelde, front towards the high-road Glasow—Lichtenrade. The particulars of occupation will be indicated on the spot by the Major of the General Staff.

From the Reserve at Dahlewitz,

> The Uhlan Regiment,
> The Fusilier Battalion of the 60th Infantry Regiment,
> The Engineer Company,

take the Blankenfelde road.

The bridge over the stream will be removed, the Battalion leaves a Company in the little wood close to the west of it, and remains with 2 guns in Blankenfelde.

The Artillery of the Reserve and the Cuirassier Regiment move by Glasow to the rendezvous. Time of starting from Dahlewitz, 4 a.m.

The Main Body follows by Glasow. Time of starting from Gross Kienitz, 4.30 a.m.

Both bridges at Glasow remain for the present occupied by small Infantry Detachments.

The Rear Guard starts from Klein Kienitz at 5 a.m., and leaves only a Cavalry post there to observe the approach of the enemy. It marches by Gross Kienitz on Glasow, and prepares for defence beyond that village.

It is also specially communicated to the Commander of the Rear Guard that an eventual retreat will be effected, according to circumstances, on Spandau or on Potsdam, that the Rear Guard has to draw the enemy at Glasow into an action which should, as much as possible, develop into a general action, that it has itself to retire in the direction of Lichtenrade, and that it should draw the enemy in the same direction. As soon as this succeeds, the Division will assume the offensive against any body that has crossed the stream.

In case of success, the Rear Guard will try to rejoin the Division on the battlefield ; otherwise it will do so northwards round Mahlow.

The Commander of the 35th Regiment receives the order to occupy Gross Beeren to-morrow morning with one Battalion, with the other, Heinersdorf, as an eventual support for the Division.

The Engineer Company after destroying the bridge of the Blankenfeld road will be ordered to march to Gross Beeren, and there to throw bridges across the stream.

The Trains are directed to Giesendorf.

The General Staff Officer has to arrange the rendezvous position so that it is entirely withdrawn from the enemy's view. Two Batteries are to be placed under cover in the salient patches of wood.

SOLUTION OF THE 34TH PROBLEM.

The Northern Division will have occupied a "position o readiness" behind Lichterfelde, as this is the most feasible, in order to be able to deploy either on the left wing towards Steglitz or on the right near the little Giesendorf wood.

In presence of the United Southern Corps it is confined to the defensive, but neither with a part nor with the whole of its strength will that Corps be able to enter Berlin without the Northern Division at once acting offensively and severing all our communications. This Division therefore must necessarily first be attacked and driven across the Havel. To force it against this river, cutting off at the same time its retreat on Potsdam and on Spandau, is certainly desirable, but hardly practicable ; the enemy is therefore to be pushed towards Potsdam, if feasible, since from Spandau he could immediately on the following day again act effectively on our flank.

The point is, to make him suffer a real defeat. The strength of the Corps permits us to attack on a front which the enemy is unable to keep occupied.

The Detachment before Berlin during the advance of the Corps remains in observation at Tempelhof.

The Advanced Guard starts at 5 a.m. for Giesendorf and prepares to cross the bridge, but awaits the attack of the Main Body before actually doing so.

The Main Body starts at 5 a.m. from the bivouac, and marches by Marienfelde and Lankwitz, the Reserve at the same hour by Lichtenrade and Mariendorf. Deployment of both columns at the Steglitzer Fichten Berg, facing west.

The attack on Steglitz will be made about 10 o'clock, and is to be supported by the simultaneous advance of the Advanced Guard on Lichterfelde. The Cavalry Regiment is to be drawn in from Berlin, and, with the Reserve Cavalry (altogether 12 Squadrons), passes between Steglitz and Dahlem to bar the enemy's retreat on Schloss Grunewald and to pursue him across the open.

Verbal remark of General von Moltke ; that the task of the Southern Corps can hardly at all any longer be executed, after the Northern Division has reached its flanking position; that under all circumstances 18,000 men were not sufficient to enter Berlin, and that, to make this probable, a much larger body had to be supposed ; but that the solution essentially depended only on the attitude of both bodies of troops.

SOLUTION OF THE 35TH PROBLEM.

If the enemy intends to maintain himself in the position, very strong in itself, on the left bank of the Mosel behind Trier, he can base himself only on the road to Prüm. Then he gives up the junction with his reinforcements, which is for him a vital object.

Wittlich is the natural point for this junction. The enemy will therefore place himself on the Coblenz road, and try to maintain himself in front of, or at least near, Wittlich.

The Corps can turn this position on the left flank, if it marches by Thalfang on Berncastel, but to do so requires at least three days, and runs the risk of being obliged to force, on the fourth day, the difficult passage across the Mosel against the enemy, who has already been reinforced. Besides, it would have to leave a Detachment against Trier in order to secure the communications with its own country and the investment of Saarlouis.

It is therefore more correct to make use of the existing superiority as soon as possible.

Our advance by Conz drives the enemy back on his reinforcements, and allows him to make full use of all the advantages of the ground in the narrow valley of the Mosel.

The enemy cannot keep Trier itself, but the further advance from there is extremely difficult for us and without danger for him, if he occupies Quint and Schweich in good time.

A direct advance against Schweich on our part obliges the enemy to evacuate the defiles of Trier, Ehrang, and Quint at once with his main forces, and to retire nearly as far as Hetzerath.

The Mosel at Schweich cannot be reached in one march, nor can it be if one wished to go by Trier, where the road would be under fire from the other bank.

The nearest road just passable for service wagons leads from Saarburg by Zerf, along the high ridge to Filsch and down to Casel. Reconnaissance of the enemy must then show whether one can get into the plain towards Schweich at Ruwer, Kenn, or Kirsch, in order to bridge across the river under cover of strong Batteries on the heights of this side.

I would therefore propose (by merely observing with patrols towards Conz and Igel) to march with the Corps to-morrow by Zerf on Pellingen.

The Advanced Guard, at the most 3 Battalions, 1 Squadron, and 2 guns, throws the outposts, which the enemy may have pushed forward, back on Feyen ; its Main Guard remains at Nieder Mennig.

The rest of the Corps, 16 Battalions, 11 Squadrons, 46 guns, and the Pontoon train, turns to the right before reaching Pellingen and bivouacs east of Filsch, as much as possible covered in the Ruwer valley.

The day after to-morrow the Advanced Guard demonstrates against Trier, occupies the enemy there, and tries to hold him fast. Should he have already evacuated the neighbourhood, it rejoins the Corps by Ehrang, or supports its attack.

The passage at Schweich is to be prepared by gun-emplacements on the height west of Kirsch as well as in the plain, and to be supported by ferrying Infantry across at Longuich. When advancing, the Reserve Artillery will therefore follow immediately behind the newly-formed Advanced Guard of the Main Body.

All further arrangements must be left to the Commander on the spot, after taking note of the enemy's measures.

SOLUTION OF THE 36TH PROBLEM.

Movements parallel with the Mosel can only be effected either in its valley or on the main ridge of the neighbouring range of heights, their slopes being impracticable for large bodies of troops. Should such a body descend to the river at any point and the valley be blocked, it cannot reach any other point on it, except by a very roundabout way.

The Mosel itself forms a barrier of the valley at its bend from Quint to Schweich.

A position for the Division, there, is supplied with that obstacle in front, which is always desirable for the weaker side ; the right wing leans against the strong defile of Quint, the right flank—the very one whence reinforcements are expected—cannot be endangered. Perpendicular to the front, two high-roads lead to the rear. Only the left wing is assailable ; but since the enemy can only ferry across or pass over by a bridge, it is in our power to break off the action at any moment so as to resume the retreat without danger. In any case the enemy is to be delayed here for a day.

I would not evacuate Trier so summarily on the 2nd May.

A Detachment of one Battalion, $\frac{1}{4}$ a 4-pr. Battery (a troop of Cavalry for observation against Conz) will render the enemy's debouching from Pallien a matter of considerable difficulty.

On the 3rd, of course the Detachment would have to be withdrawn, if the enemy does not attack by Trier in a westerly direction. But it need not be withdrawn at once beyond the Quint ; rather will the $\frac{1}{4}$ Battery find an opportunity for taking up flanking positions in the plain of Pfalzel and Ehrang, which will incommode the enemy very much indeed in his attack on our front.

The rest of the Division goes back on Schweich on the 2nd May.

We cannot enter upon a real duel with the enemy's Artillery, which is double our strength. In general, our Batteries will have to be placed about 1,800 paces in rear of the Mosel, so as to escape the greatest effect of the enemy's fire, but to keep the river still under an effective fire, as well as the construction of the bridge in all probability intended to be effected there. A Battery, however, will have to be built where the road from Trier leaves the Quint defile, whence the river can be enfiladed.

Quint is to be occupied by 2 Companies, Schweich by 4 ; 6 Companies go to the Mehringer Berg, to observe as far as Mehring, and prevent the crossing of small hostile bodies.

The Reserves, 6 Battalions and the Cavalry on the covered ground north of Issel, assume the offensive when the passage is being effected, and the hostile Artillery is at least partly masked thereby. But I hardly believe that the enemy can force a passage here.

SOLUTION OF THE 37TH PROBLEM.

If it were wished to continue the march on Berlin and to confine oneself to leave behind a body of about equal strength for observation of the enemy, the Division would be too weak for entering a large city.

If we succeeded in throwing the enemy across the Spree and destroying the bridge, the latter could be barred with little effort, and also a renewed advance of the enemy prevented at Schmöckwitz and Cöpenick.

It would, however, be indisputably the most advantageous to force a battle upon the enemy and to annihilate him with our superior strength.

If the Division advances on the 2nd June by Schenkendorf—Krummensee, the enemy can, in order to evade the fight, bring his troops from Königs-Wusterhausen and Senzig by Neue Mühle in safety behind the Spree; but he can also concentrate the whole in a very strong position between Königs and Deutsch Wusterhausen, which is difficult to force from the south. If this succeeds, he is after all only pushed back on Berlin.

If we advance by Ragow north round the bog, the enemy will find south of Königs-Wusterhausen a far less strong position, which can probably be forced by superior numbers. But he will defend it only with his Rear Guard, and give way with his Main Body to the south. A further pursuit draws the Division completely away from its real object, without giving it the certainty of bringing the enemy to bay anywhere, owing to the superiority of his Cavalry.

If we then wish to return from Wusterhausen and march on Berlin, the enemy will at once follow, interrupt all communications, and place us in the most awkward position between an unbeaten enemy and the hostile capital.

According to my opinion there remains only an advance with the Division south of the bog on the 2nd June. If the enemy withdraws behind the Spree, Neue Mühle will be occupied, the bridge there destroyed, and the march continued on Berlin by König-Wus-terhausen.

If the enemy gives way by Senzig, the whole Division will follow, and there is then every prospect of beating him at Bindow, Gussow, or Prieros.

If, however, as is probable, he takes up the position at Wuster-hausen, the bridge at Neue Mühle is to be destroyed and his debouching towards the south to be rendered as difficult as possible by abattis, gun-emplacements, etc.

This ground remains occupied by the Advanced Guard, 3 Battalions, 1 Battery, and ½ a Squadron. The Main Body has not followed further than is necessary, probably not beyond the line Schenkendorf—Krummensee. It starts early on the 3rd, marches through and alongside Mittenwalde on Ragow, in the direction of Hoherlehme—a march of seven miles—and attacks the enemy as soon as possible, if he tries to break through to the south, or gives way to the north.

SOLUTION OF THE 38TH PROBLEM.

The march of the enemy over the mountains cannot be executed in one day, particularly if he encounters some resistance.

It must further be made in separate columns, if one will not run the risk of seeing all brought to a stand by resistance at *one* point.

In order to debouch simultaneously with these columns, the Main Body of the enemy will, on the 2nd May, move up to the line Suhl—Zella—Mehlis—Benshausen—Schmalkalden, which are the only places where billets are to be found.

From there to the open plain the distance is, on the average, 12 to 14 miles by the nearest roads, which lead into the line Frankenhain—Waltershausen.

If the enemy turns further east, he can debouch only on the 4th May; if he takes a more westerly direction, he endangers his communications without threatening ours with Erfurt.

The Division will concentrate around Ohrdruf, where it has the best lateral communications, in order to throw itself with *all available* forces upon one of the debouching columns. But at the same time the advance of the others must still be hindered as much as possible in the mountains.

The barriers, there, are] situated close to, but beyond, the Rennsteig. The Advanced Guards of the enemy will thus try to get hold of them as early as the 2nd May. The Division will therefore concentrate early in the morning of the 2nd May. It forms 3 Advanced Guards, each consisting of 1 Battalion of the 31st Regiment, two 4-pr. guns of Battery No. 1, some troopers as orderlies, and a Detachment of Engineers.

The Advanced Guards move along the roads by Tambach, Oberhof, and Schmücke, as far as the Rennsteig, on which they seek connection, observe to the left and right, but occupy difficult passes forward, and attempt to defend them obstinately. Resistance will also be continued in the valleys of the northern slopes of the mountains, in order to ensure that one or the other column will debouch later than the rest.

The General of Division will then base his determination for the offensive on the reports coming in from the Advanced Guards.

He will, at the same time, have to consider that a rush of hostile columns against his left wing would threaten his communications with Erfurt more than one would against his right wing, or a turning movement round the latter, perhaps by Friedrichsroda or Brotterode, to which place he will detach a party only for observation.

SOLUTION OF THE 39TH PROBLEM.

A hostile Brigade is beaten, and its reappearance is not to be expected in the immediate future.

But if the enemy is 24,000 strong he can now have assembled 18,000 on this side of the mountains. If we attack these behind the Apfelstedt with 13,000 we shall, in case of mishap, be thrown back in an easterly direction, and Erfurt, which is not yet defensible, runs the risk of being taken by assault.

I would decide for the defensive and take post west of Arnstadt.

The enemy has on the 2nd May marched and fought till evening; he can undertake nothing more on that day; yet neither can we execute a march, but only start early in the morning.

The enemy is as close to Arnstadt as we are, but it is not at all to be assumed that he will summarily march on Erfurt, knowing us to be in his rear at Elgersburg. He will without doubt march first in that direction, if it were only to disengage his 4th Brigade and to draw it in again if possible.

Only the 2 Battalions at Ohrdruf, therefore, which are too much exposed, will be recalled on the 3rd, that is to say, to Wölfis.

At 4 o'clock a.m., on the 4th, the 12th Hussar Regiment advances by Angelroda, Liebenstein, towards Wölfis, to pick up the 2 Battalions, and to observe the further march of the enemy. These 2 Battalions, 5 Squadrons, and 4 4-prs. withdraw, if pressed, by the Tambusch on Bittstedt.

The Regiment No. 71 and 2 4-pr. guns, as a flank guard, follow the Hussars as far as Liebenstein, and strike out thence in the direction of Vw. Eikfeld, yet so slowly, that they still cover the rear of the Main Body, which moves on the high-road by Plaue, through and round Arnstadt, into a covered bivouac behind the Pfennigs Berg.

The 2 6-pr. Batteries move at once up to the height mentioned and prepare gun-emplacements. All the rest holds itself in readiness to deploy to the left or right of this Artillery position, according to how the enemy advances.

SOLUTION OF THE 40TH PROBLEM.

I.

Only 2 Battalions of the Advanced Guard with some Cavalry detachments remain in the town during the night. The 3rd Rifle Battalion occupies the railway station with 1 Company, and the northern exit of the town with 1 Company, to which are attached 2 guns ; 2 Companies bivouac in the market-place. The outposts are pushed out only 500 to 600 paces, the nearest ground is to be reconnoitred by continual patrolling, but the enemy is not to be alarmed. The 1st Battalion of the 5th Regiment will be sheltered in alarm-houses. The rest of the Advanced Guard bivouacs close behind the town south of the Spree. The 2nd Battalion will furnish 1 officer and 50 men as a guard for the bridge.

2.

DISPOSITION FOR THE 1ST APRIL.

Headquarters, Ketschendorf,

31st March, 1870, 9 p.m.

The 3rd Brigade will to-morrow form the Advanced Guard. It starts at 6 a.m., and takes possession of the vineyards near Vw. Fürstenwalde.

At the same hour will stand :

The 1st Brigade on the Langenwahl road,

„ 2nd „ „ „ Rauen „

the Cavalry Brigade between both, all 1,000 paces this side of the Spree bridge in rendezvous formation ready to start. The Reserve Artillery moves into a position on the left bank of the Spree east of the suburb. Should the enemy offer resistance to the Advanced Guard, the 1st Brigade will first defile, further orders being held over. If, on the contrary, the enemy continues his retreat, about which the Advanced Guard has to report without delay, the Cavalry Brigade with the Batteries will advance first to reinforce it. Colonel N. takes command of the Advanced Guard Cavalry, has to overtake the enemy and force him to fight, if possible, on the open ground this side of Müncheberg. The 2nd Brigade then defiles behind the Cavalry, and marches, without waiting for the 1st Brigade, by Bärenfelde and Schönfelde ; the 1st Brigade with the Corps Reserve Artillery follows the Advanced Guard on the road by Gölsdorf. The General commanding is with the 1st Infantry Brigade.

SOLUTION OF THE 41ST PROBLEM.

If the Division deploys where it is in bivouac, it will find in its front an exceedingly strong position between Dahmsdorf and Maus Bridge. It is not to be apprehended that the enemy will turn this position on the left ; he would thereby expose his own communications and commit himself to very difficult ground. On the other hand, it is probable that he will advance on our right flank through the Sieversdorfer Forst, thus threatening the retreat to the high-road and forcing us away towards the north, where the line of communication of the 3rd Division would then no longer be protected. The direction taken to-day by a hostile column to Schönfelde seems to indicate this intention.

We shall therefore be obliged to occupy with the Main Body of the Division at once that position, in which we will offer resistance, and this can only be the height on which the road from Berg Schäferei stretches to Vw. Abendroth. It can only be attacked in front, and under the fire of the Reserve Artillery to be placed there. Intermediate positions in advance of this position are not to be recommended. The ground nowhere admits of the full deployment of the Division, and it would run the risk of being hustled on to the main position.

On the other hand, the Rear Guard finds on this very ground everywhere opportunity of hampering the march of the enemy and securing ours ; only it must not withdraw on the main position, but, unmasking it, has to turn north of Buckow to Bollersdorf. The enemy can hardly risk a serious attack on the Main Body before pushing back the Detachment standing at that moment on his right flank. Its withdrawal, when finally forced by superior numbers, will be favoured exceedingly by the ground, the enemy will be turned off in a direction advantageous to us, and his advance retarded by continually renewed small Rear Guard actions. At Bollersdorf the Rear Guard covers the line of communications, and the junction of the former with its Main Body under cover of the Cavalry Division, which is to be stationed at Hasenholz, can hardly be endangered. The enemy has to march, continually fighting, 9 miles to Bollersdorf, and it is very doubtful whether he will gain any ground to-morrow. Should he still succeed in penetrating at Bollersdorf or Berg Shäferei, the junction with the Division will take place behind the obstacle of Garzin. It remains to be considered that the direction of the enemy's attack through the Sieversdorfer Forst is certainly probable, but that he can also advance from Müncheberg by the high-road and the road parallel to it.

I accordingly propose the following :

The Rear Guard : Infantry Regiment No. 41, Rifle Battalion No. 1, 1st 4-pr. Battery, and 2 Squadrons Dragoons, stand at 4 a.m. under cover behind Schlagenthin. The Rifle Battalion occupies Dahmsdorf with 1 Company, the lake defile with 1 Section, to which 2 guns will be attached, and the Maus Bridge with 1 Section. It is in the power of the Commander of the Rear Guard to reinforce rapidly these points since the hostile advance can be perfectly overlooked. The Fusilier Battalion and 1 Squadron are detached to Neubodengrün and the Strill Berg (east of Hoppegarten). They reconnoitre towards Schönfelde and Eggersdorf.

The Cavalry Division halts at 5 o'clock north of Dahmsdorf, and reconnoitres towards Müncheberg. The Main Body starts also at 5 a.m., retreating by the high-road, first the Trains, which continue to march as far as Garzin, then the Artillery, which moves into position on the heights already mentioned, then the 1st Brigade follows.

To carry out this withdrawal undisturbed, by one road, $1\frac{1}{2}$ hours are needed, which the resistance of the Rear Guard must procure. Its conduct will be determined by the reports from Dahmsdorf and Neubodengrün respectively. If the enemy advances between Rothe Luch and Gumnitz, the Cavalry Division, which is to be apprised immediately, marches by the Buckow road, then south round the Schermützel See to Hasenholz. The Infantry of the Rear Guard moves by the road leading from Schlagenthin to Hoppegarten, in order to pick up the Fusilier Battalion No. 41, but the Squadron and the Battery by the high-road direct, as far as over the bridge at Wüsten Sieversdorf, where the whole Rear Guard then will again assemble in order to continue the retreat on Buckow, fighting in the manner already indicated.

SOLUTION OF THE 42ND PROBLEM.

The 6th Brigade is summoned early (4 o'clock) to Vw. Anitz by Garzau, the Division holding the position of Garzin until its arrival. The two 6-pr. Batteries move up to the heights south-east of Hohenstein, which flank this position. The 1st Infantry Brigade occupies the crest on this side of the valley, and the village of Garzin, the 2nd Brigade with the 4-pr. Battery stands in reserve covered in the valley west of Garzin Mill. The Dragoon Regiment halts behind Hohenstein, both Uhlan Regiments and the Cuirassier Regiment place themselves under cover behind the wood east of Vw. Anitz. From there the offensive will be assumed as soon as the enemy is engaged and the 6th Brigade has arrived. Should the enemy turn our position north by Ruhlsdorf, the 2nd Brigade goes to meet him between Hohenstein and the 6-pr. Batteries ; the 1st Brigade joins by Garzin the advance of the 6th Brigade and of the Cavalry Division on Liebenhof. It is also possible that the enemy on the 3rd April altogether gives up further pursuit, in order to join the Main Army before Berlin, whereby we shall then be in possession of the shorter route to Berlin. If no attack ensues till 8 o'clock, the Cavalry with the Horse Artillery, and one Battalion, advance against the Berg Schäferei. The latter drives in the enemy's posts and reconnoitres the march of the enemy. The Cavalry eventually follows his movements north of the Rothe Luch, and stations itself for observation towards Heidekrug. The 6th Brigade takes the direction from Anitz by Zinndorf on Herzfelde, where it remains as a Rear Guard. The

Division marches by Hennickendorf, the Trains by Forsthaus Schlag
to Tasdorf, into bivouac. By holding this defile, Berlin can then be
reached in one march, and sooner than by the enemy. An offensive
over the difficult ground of Buckow I do not consider advisable, as
even in case of success it only drives the hostile Corps back on the
Main Body of its Army, but separates us from Berlin, where,
probably, all forces are wanted for a decisive battle.

SOLUTION OF THE 43RD PROBLEM.

I.

The Division has two things to keep in view: firstly, the bringing up of the reinforcements into Belfort, but then also the securing
of the concentration at Mülhausen during the 4th March, on which
day the 28th Division cannot yet undertake this.

Both objects are attained if one prevents the enemy from debouching from the mountains. This he can only do on two roads: by
Thann or by Giromagny. The valley of Massevaux*, according to
the map, cannot be used by large bodies.

The road by Giromagny leads the enemy straight to Belfort.
He is obliged to make a detour which, towards the left, is rendered
difficult by the wood d'Arsot, and towards the right costs him two
marches, in order to turn the fortress on the south.

Advancing by Thann, however, the enemy can, as regards time,
have reached the neighbourhood of Felleringen—St. Amarin, by the
3rd March, and on the 4th can threaten the communication between
Mülhausen and Belfort.

To hinder this the Division needs all its forces. It will therefore
advance on the 4th with its full strength against Thann, but despatch
the convoy and the Landwehr on the road by Altkirch to Dannemarie,† which, owing to the Rhone Canal and the distance, is the
most secure.

In a defensive position between Auberge de la Croisière and
Aspach le Haut it will render the deployment of even superior
hostile forces exceedingly difficult, secure the detraining at Merxheim and Mülhausen, and cover the march of the convoy.

By the energy with which the enemy tries to debouch it will be

---

* Masmünster.   † Dammerkirch.

recognised whether one has to deal here with his main force. In such a case the Division will certainly have also to maintain its position on the 5th March until it is strengthened or relieved by the 28th Division. But then the march of the convoy to Belfort will be free from danger on that day.

If, however, on the 4th March the enemy's attack is beaten off with ease, or does not take place at all, it may be expected that he has taken the direction of Giromagny with his Main Body.

In that case the 28th Division must undertake the observation of the mountain-road by occupying Cernay,* but the 29th Division, while securing its right flank by an Infantry Flank Guard, must advance by La Chapelle and St. Germain, in order to cover the march of the convoy according to circumstances.

If the enemy were not yet near, the Division could, by occupying the wood d'Arsot, take up an Advanced Guard position for the advance of the Army ; if the enemy has already debouched in superior numbers there remains for the Division the retreat behind the Rhone Canal.

2.

DISPOSITION FOR THE 4TH MARCH.

Mülhausen, 3rd March, 6 p.m.

The Division starts to-morrow, the 4th March, at 6 a.m., in two columns, in the direction of Thann.

> 1st column : 57th Brigade, 3rd and 4th light Batteries, and 2nd Engineer Company,

on the road by Pfastadt and Lutterbach. It reconnoitres the Nonnenbruch by skirmishers, who, as soon as possible, occupy the north-western edge of the wood.

> 2nd column : 58th Brigade, 3rd and 4th heavy Batteries, and 3rd Engineer Company,

by Nieder Morschwiller and Renningen to Aspach. Its Advanced Guard will be formed by the Fusilier Battalion of Regiment No. 17; the Artillery march behind the 2nd Battalion of this Regiment.

The Dragoon Regiment places itself at the head of the 1st column but leaves the high-road at Lutterbach, advances at a trot,

---

* Sennheim.

leaving the Nonnenbruch to the right, reconnoitres against Vieux Thann,* and reports to both columns.

Only two Ambulance Detachments from the Train will follow.

The convoy which is intended for Belfort marches on the 4th under escort of the Landwehr and of the Cavalry orderlies attached to it, by Altkirch to Dannemarie, and, if no special obstacles are met, continues the march from there to Belfort on the 5th.

The Divisional Commander reserves to himself to order verbally :

If the Dragoon Regiment does not encounter the enemy to-morrow when reconnoitring, the Fusilier Battalion of Regiment No. 17 enters Thann and patrols by Willer. The Division goes into close cantonments on the line Cernay—Michelbach, and secures itself by outposts towards the mountains.

If, however, the Cavalry meets the enemy already in the act of debouching the Division will attack him unhesitatingly and throw him back into the defile.

To this end the 57th Brigade deploys to the left at Ochsenfeld, the 58th Brigade to the right in advance of Aspach le Haut. The latter occupies at once with both heavy Batteries and the Fusilier Battalion of the 17th Regiment the height north-west of this village.

3.

The Commandant of Belfort is to be informed of the march of the convoy. He is requested to detach a party towards the latter, and to occupy if possible the wood d'Arsot.

Report to the headquarters of the 14th Army Corps on the intended advance of the Division, and request to have Cernay occupied by the 28th Division as early as possible on the 5th March.

SOLUTION OF THE 44TH PROBLEM.

The investment of Belfort towards the east cannot be carried out as long as there is a hostile Division close to the place in the open field.

If success is at all to be gained it can only be by the Corps assuming the offensive before larger hostile masses concentrate, therefore without delay and with all available forces. The investment of the west front of the fortress will therefore be confined at first to a mere observation, in order to prevent any requisitioning in the neighbouring country.

* Alt Thann.

To turn Belfort in the south would cost two days, and in the north the only available road is that by Magny and Anjoutey, as the valley of Offemont is thoroughly commanded by the fort la Miotte.

The following is proposed :

The 11th Infantry Regiment, with ⅓ Battery No. 5, advances by the road towards Belfort, occupies the height north of Valdoye, clears the wood d'Arsot from the enemy, and observes the fortress.

The rest of the 3rd Division : the 5th Infantry Brigade, with 2 Batteries, strengthened by the 2nd Hussar Regiment, forms the Advanced Guard, and marches by Magny, Etueffont, and Anjoutey, occupies St. Germain, reconnoitres with the Cavalry the ground lying ahead, and occupies the bridge over the Madelaine brook.

The 2nd Division, and then the 2nd Cavalry Brigade, follow at short distances as soon as the road is clear. The former moves from Anjoutey south towards Menoncourt, the latter halts until further orders at Anjoutey.

The 1st Division detaches the 4th Infantry Regiment with the 1st Battery from Ronchamp by Frahier to Chalonvillars. It is joined by the 1st Hussar Regiment from Giromagny, by Chaux and Errevet. The detachment is charged with observing the west front of the fortress without exposing itself to its fire, and puts itself, by Mont Salbert, into communication with the post before Valdoye.

The rest of the Division advances from Champagney by Auxelles, Giromagny towards Gros Magny. The Division will find there the order whether it is to continue the march or to cook.

All the columns will start simultaneously (6 a.m.)

Although the 2nd and 3rd Divisions have only to march 9 miles, as far as beyond Anjoutey, they cannot be counted upon being assembled there sooner than midday, as there is only one mountain road available.

If the enemy is met he will be attacked without hesitation, and also the 1st Division be ordered up.

If the enemy gives way the pursuit cannot be carried far on that day.

If the enemy is not discovered, the position St. Germain—Menoncourt becomes, by securing the only road for retreat, suitable for meeting by a flank attack the advance of the enemy, be that on the northern road by Soppe or the southern by Altkirch.

SOLUTION OF THE 45TH PROBLEM.

To the Commanders of the 28th, 29th, 30th Infantry, and of the
Cavalry Division (identical).

Mülhausen, 5th March, 6 p.m.

In case of an attack by the enemy in superior numbers the 29th
Division continues its retreat to-morrow, the 6th March, from Traubach by Balschwiller to Spechbach le Haut, behind which place it will
then take up a position.   Since, however, it is desirable to draw the
enemy in that direction the Rear Guard will fight where it is standing ;
the Division will provide for intermediate positions as far as may be
required for the Rear Guard to fall back upon.   It will then send in
advance both heavy Batteries, which will unlimber on the height east
of Spechbach le Haut.   The Division keeps the village occupied, deploys with the Main Body on the high ridge to the right of the Battery
with the right wing touching the road from Bernwiller to Galfingen.
The Rear Guard rallies as a Reserve on the reverse slope of the heights.

The 30th Division will advance at 6 a.m. from Mülhausen by
Galfingen.   It deploys for action on the height between the road
already indicated and the Freywald, occupying the latter with
skirmishers.

Both Divisions send forward their whole Artillery ; the Infantry
and, behind it, the Divisional Cavalry, place themselves in a position
covered by the height.   The details of occupation I shall arrange on
the spot.

The 28th Division also starts at 6 a.m. from Cernay, and forms
up in rendezvous position under cover behind Burnhaupt le Bas.   It
puts itself into communication with the 30th Division through the
Freywald, and observes through the Langelittenhaag towards Soppe.

The Cavalry Division assembles in the clearing of the wood east
of Burnhaupt, the Corps Artillery south of Galfingen.

It is intended, as soon as the enemy is engaged in front of the
29th and 30th Divisions, to attack his flank with the 28th Division.

Should he advance by Soppe, the offensive will be assumed from
the direction of our left wing.

I shall stop during the fight on the height south of Galfingen.

If the enemy to-morrow should not attack at all seriously, the
Advanced Guard of the 29th Division will maintain its position in
advance of Traubach.

The further orders are to be issued in accordance with the above.

SOLUTION OF THE 46TH AND 47TH PROBLEMS.

Shorthand report of the verbal criticism of General v. Moltke.

In the first problem (46) I had set my eye upon a flanking position, the special occupation of which was required in the following problem.

Where it is not absolutely necessary to hold on to a distinct line of operation, as in an enemy's country, one can change one's base of operation according to circumstances,—therefore, remove the line of retreat either to fortresses or to one's own bodies of troops. Here, there was no necessity for holding on to the road to Berlin ; the 2nd Corps rather presented the most natural objective for a retreat, and support was to be expected from it.

But if it is desired to occupy a flanking position, one cannot form up on an open plain, perhaps parallel to the road by which the advance of the enemy is expected, for otherwise the enemy would attack the nearest wing and gain for himself the full effect of a flank attack. A flanking position must rather be chosen so that with the wings leaning as much as possible on strong points it can have a surprising effect.

All this the 5th Division will find in the position Arensdorf— Falkenhagen. We may bet a hundred to one that the enemy who has followed us for 3 or 4 days in a distinct direction will continue his advance for the present in the same direction,—namely, by the high-road Müncheberg—Berlin. Now, in order to confirm him in the assumption that he will still meet the 5th Division on that road, a Rear Guard, strength : 1 Battalion of Infantry, the whole of the Cavalry and 1 Battery, should remain as outposts near Petershagen, retire at the approach of the enemy, and only at Georgenthal offer serious resistance until the enemy arrives within the effective fire of the Batteries of the Main Body, so as then rapidly to clear the front of the Division by retreating on Arensdorf.

The rest of the Division occupies the following position : The 3 Batteries north-west of the defile between Schmerlen and Kalk See ; 1 Regiment of the 9th Brigade north-west of Georgenthal, the other north-west of it in reserve ; the 10th Brigade north-west of Hinterste Graning ; the Rifle Battalion at the defiles of Falkenhagen.

If the enemy's Advanced Guard follows our Rear Guard beyond Georgenthal, it is taken under effective fire and obliged to give way to the south towards Wilmersdorf.

H

The Main Body of the enemy has a threefold choice : 1. It gives way to the north to get thereby into the rear of our position. (It is assumed here that it has precise intelligence from its Advanced Guard.) The enemy will not do this, however, for he will thereby be in danger of being attacked sideways by the 2nd Corps, and he entirely loses connection with his Advanced Guard. 2. The Main Body continues to advance by the road ; then the Division attains its object. 3. The Main Body bends towards the south, to attack our front, together with its Advanced Guard ; but then it has at its disposal only the roads by Madlitz and Briesen. The former is, however, not suitable for the use of the Main Body of an Army Corps. It will therefore have to sweep round by Briesen ; that is 13 miles. It is doubtful whether the enemy will still be able to attack after marching 13 miles. If he does so, the Division stands opposite him in a favourable position, completely rested, with its line of retreat on the 2nd Army Corps, from which it can receive support.

If the enemy does not attack we have gained a day, and operations can be mutually arranged with the 2nd Army Corps. The enemy is thereby in a position of having entirely deviated from his line of retreat. This is for him the more disadvantageous, as his base lies very near. For the Frankfurt Oder bridge forms here his base exclusively ; it has shrunk to this one point.

SOLUTION OF THE 48TH PROBLEM.

Shorthand report of the verbal criticism of General v. Moltke.

The situation of the enemy is given in the problem as clearly as it can really be wished for. It is certain that the greater part of the enemy, which had followed our Corps, has disappeared from Sonnenburg ; it is also to be assumed with certainty that on the 2nd March only weak hostile forces were concentrated on the left bank of the Oder. The enemy has not tried to turn us out for good at Trepplin, consequently, he thinks himself not strong enough to attack. Further, no attempt has been made to cross the Oder between Cüstrin and Lebus. Such a crossing is also not so quickly effected. Our skirmishers, who are lying behind the Oder embankments, must above all be driven away by the enemy, and he must commence a cannonade before he can think at all about constructing a bridge.

An offensive on our part is therefore advisable. One must

decidedly make use of the time and opportunity for making our momentary superiority felt. One could without doubt retire unmolested on this day (3rd March), and concentrate all forces perhaps in the neighbourhood of Heinersdorf and Müncheberg, but then one would have to oppose, on the 4th March, the same superiority on the left bank of the Oder which one could not cope with on the right bank.

The majority of gentlemen have accordingly proceeded offensively, and led their forces forward as they were standing at the moment, viz.: the 2nd Corps on Schönfliess and the 5th Division on Boosen. But one must be clear at the same time how the enemy will act. If we succeed in attacking him on two sides and in effecting the junction of two columns on the battlefield, the greatest results are certainly to be expected. So we have done, for example, at Königgrätz in 1866. But is it permissible to suppose this here? No! The enemy will evade such an attack or assume the offensive himself, in order to fall upon one of our separate bodies with superior numbers.

The latter must be assumed as the more likely, because it is for him a question of procuring room for the troops which have crossed the river.

The position between Malnow and the Aalkasten See has an extent of little over a mile; it can therefore just be occupied by a Division. The 4th Division, of which the 8th Brigade is already in Dolgelin as an Advanced Guard, must be formed up there; the 3rd Division will be assembled behind it at Karzig—Alter Weinberg. Finally, the 5th Division is to close in. Its Rear Guard holds for this purpose the road defile on the Treppliner See. One Brigade will march straight by Falkenhagen to Hohen Jesar, the other advances to Petershagen, in order to support at first the very isolated Rear Guard and to prevent the enemy from advancing to the west. This Brigade then also goes to Hohen Jesar, and the Advanced Guard follows it there by Sieversdorf and Wald Mill. I would fix the times by ordering the Divisions to have reached the positions mentioned at 9 o'clock; the Divisions will calculate accordingly their own hours of starting. The troops can start in March at 6 o'clock.

If the enemy advances on Trepplin and Falkenhagen he will deliver a blow into the air. If he turns towards Hohen Jesar against the 5th Division, the 2nd Corps will attack him.

H 2

If he turns straight to the north the 5th Division advances against his flank. The latter will have placed its Artillery on the heights south of Hohen Jesar, and sweep with its fire the ground towards Wulkow and Schönfliess. It also occupies Alt Zeschdorf and the little wood north of it. Thus we can, after a defensive attitude, assume a successful offensive. Everything seems to warrant that we can occupy the position. Wüst Kunersdorf is not much nearer to the Aalkasten See than Dolgelin, and Frankfurt not nearer than Seelow. It is always most essential to make dispositions for only so much as can be executed with certainty. The General commanding will be at the north-east corner of the Aalkasten See, whence to the nearest Divisional Commander it is only about a mile.

SOLUTION OF THE 49TH PROBLEM.

Shorthand report of the verbal criticism of General v. Moltke.

The problem was one of a nature purely editorial. Three questions were concerned here: *To whom? What? How?* Brevity is herein absolutely necessary, but completeness the main thing.

1. To Whom?

Is an order to be sent also to the 2nd and 4th Army Corps? A mistake it would not be, for one cannot be too strong at the decisive moment. But neither is it absolutely necessary; for it was said in the problem : only those Corps should be summoned up which could reach the battlefield in the course of that day. If one wished to do so, one Division of the 4th Corps would for instance be ordered up to Thiaucourt, the 2nd Corps to the bridges at Corny and Arry. The 2nd Corps must not go to Pont-à-Mousson, because from the direction of Corny and Arry the covering of the Mosel with its roads, as also the support of the right wing of the 2nd Army, is more easily effected.

To the Guard and 12th Army Corps orders must be sent at any rate directly from Grand Headquarters, for if they pass through the headquarters of the Army it will be too late, particularly as the quarters of the latter for the night are unknown. To the 7th and 8th Army Corps, however, no direct orders are to be issued but through the headquarters of the 1st Army, as these latter are only about 5 miles distant. The regular channels are therefore always to be made use of unless deviation therefrom becomes an urgent necessity.

This is not the case here, as the 7th and 8th Army Corps need only to start the next morning. Neither must the 9th Army Corps be immediately disposed of, as the headquarters of the Army probably have already ordered its closing up. These orders are therefore to be issued in writing to the two headquarters of the 7th and 8th, and the 2nd, 4th, and 9th Army Corps respectively, and directly by wire to the Guard and 12th Army Corps.

2. WHAT?

In the telegrams the general situation must be briefly stated. This is necessary in order to explain the change in the direction of march. This general information must be identical, if possible, so that everyone is informed of the duties of the neighbouring bodies. The 12th Cavalry Division must not be ordered directly because it is placed under the command of the 12th Army Corps, and because this Corps will have more secure and more rapid communication (Relais) with it.

The general information for the two Army Headquarters need not be identical, nor are times to be indicated for the marches, as one surely cannot calculate beforehand at the Grand Headquarters the marches of 18 to 23 miles of the different Corps. One would only unnecessarily increase one's own responsibility by such detailed arrangements. To select the various routes for marching is also the business of the chiefs of the Staffs of the Armies and Army Corps, who can have them previously reconnoitred by officers. Neither to the Guard and 12th Corps nor to the 7th and 8th are therefore distinct roads to be assigned, but only the general directions, and the objects on which to march, are to be indicated.

3. HOW?

A. *To the Headquarters of the 1st Army at Coin sur Seille.* (*By Orderly Officer.*)

Pont-à-Mousson, 16th August, 1870, 7 p.m.

3rd and 10th Corps have maintained themselves to-day west of Metz against great superiority of the enemy. Guard and 12th Corps are set in motion on Mars la Tour. The 7th and 8th Corps are to be moved up across the Mosel at Corny and Arry to the right wing of the battlefield at Vionville, but only after the 9th Corps, and by the shortest road. The Trains remain on this side of the Mosel. Ammunition Columns are to be brought up to supply the 3rd Corps also.

Reports to His Majesty are to be directed to-morrow morning to the height south of Flavigny.

B. *To the Headquarters of the 2nd Army by Novéant-Gorze.* (*In duplicate, by two Officers.*)

Pont-à-Mousson, 16th August, 1870, 7 p.m.

By wire from here the Guard and 12th Army Corps have been ordered up to Mars la Tour by Beney and Thiaucourt, the former to the left, the latter to the right; 12th Cavalry Division to advance as early as possible for observation of the roads from Etain and Briey to Metz. The 7th and 8th Corps cross the Mosel to-morrow after the 9th Corps, and move by the shortest road to the right wing of the battle-field at Vionville. His Majesty arrives to-morrow morning at the height south of Flavigny.

C. *Telegram to the Headquarters of the Guard Corps at Bernecourt.*

Pont-à-Mousson, 16th August, 1870, 7 p.m.

3rd and 10th Corps fought to-day west of Metz against a superior enemy. Guard and 12th Corps will march this night to Mars la Tour by Beney to the left and Thiaucourt to the right. 12th Cavalry Division to be moved forward against roads from Etain and Briey to Metz. Guard Uhlan Brigade remains against Maas. Bring up Ammunition Columns.

D. *Telegram to the Headquarters of the 12th Corps at Fey en Haye* (*Identical*).

SOLUTION OF THE 50TH PROBLEM.

A. *Written solution by General v. Moltke.*

A defensive position at Gumbinnen behind the Rominte and Lower Pissa would not, according to my opinion, fulfil its purpose. It precludes us from following up at once any success by an offensive movement. The fight for the town would mean its destruction. If unsuccessful we have the defiles of the Angerapp behind us. It is also possible that the enemy anticipates us in Gumbinnen.

I would propose a flanking position, with the left wing on the Angerapp, with the right on the Augskallner or Plickner Berge.

Whether the position on the heights in advance of Gerwischken—Szublauken, or one still further forward near Pagramutschen—Wilken is to be chosen, must be decided on the spot by a General Staff Officer, who is to be sent in advance with an escort. In both cases the Cavalry Division under cover behind the hills, in order to rush at the right moment upon the enemy's left flank ; the most important tactical pivots of the open front occupied by Artillery ; Infantry on the hilly ground unseen as long as possible. The Horse Artillery Batteries under Cavalry escort pushed forward against the Rominte and Pissa, to make the enemy's passage difficult and to mark it.

The enemy cannot pass our position without giving up all his communications. If he would succeed in driving us out of it, all bridges over the Angerapp from Nemmersdorf to Darkehmen can be used successively, in order to rally beyond the river again on the flank of the enemy's advance.

B. *Verbatim shorthand report of General v. Moltke's verbal criticism.*

Gentlemen, I should like, before discussing the problem with you, to make some remarks which have also a general application.

If we consider the geographical features, we see that the enemy is advancing from east to west, we from south to north. Both lines of march must therefore cross, and this they will do, if both parties continue in the direction indicated, at Gumbinnen, since both parties are equally distant from there. If we bar the enemy at Gumbinnen, we must turn to the right, and therefore shift our line of retreat from the south to the west, while the enemy retains his directly behind himself to the east. Matters are changed, if we do not march as far as Gumbinnen, but halt south of it. Thereby we oblige the enemy on his part to turn to the left, if he wishes to attack us ; he then gets his line of retreat on his left flank while ours remains behind us to the south. But the shifting of his line of retreat is much more dangerous to him than to us, as we are in our own country, while he can be forced against the Haff as occasion may arise.

One can in general deduce from this that flanking positions will mostly be taken up only in one's own country, while invading Armies can but rarely do so. This sounds somewhat abstract and academic, but it is indeed always a precarious thing in war to fight on a front reversed. We did so, it is true, on the 18th of August, 1870, but we could do it because we had gained victories on the 14th and 16th and because we had a great superiority over the enemy. Whether here the shifting of one's own line of retreat would be injurious cannot be ascertained, as it depends on many other circumstances which were not apparent from the problem.

If, now, we wish to take up such a flanking position, we must require that the flank which it presents to the enemy is resting on, or otherwise protected by, the ground, by favourable Artillery positions, or by the position of the reserve. Imagine, gentlemen, . that we take up a flanking position on perfectly open ground, the enemy would surely not do us the favour of deploying in front of us in order to attack us from there, but he would advance obliquely against the wing nearest to him and roll up our position. The right flank, which is threatened here, has a good support on the Plickner Berge. The effect of a flanking position, besides, need not alone depend on keeping the enemy's line of advance under an effective fire, but it can make itself also felt by an offensive movement from the position. This, gentlemen, is, as it were, the general skeleton around which the other measures must now arrange themselves as flesh and blood.

Those gentlemen who have marched to Gumbinnen fulfil the first part of the problem, for they bar thereby the enemy's further advance to Königsberg; but it is a question whether they have in doing so made use of all the advantages which the situation offered. It appears to me more advantageous to remain south of Gumbinnen. It certainly is not absolutely necessary for the enemy to advance by Gumbinnen; but, gentlemen, if you allow probability to have any influence, you may very well assume this. The enemy has been advancing from east to west for several days; he will therefore probably, if there are no special reasons, continue in this direction; because it is important for him to reach Gumbinnen, as he can quarter a great part of his Corps in the town and secure the defiles there. It is improbable that the enemy will evade us towards the north, because he would then have to fight on a reversed front. Such things do not happen in reality. Besides, he would be voluntarily going into the great moor and swamp district. It is most probable, therefore, that he advances on Gumbinnen. If, now, we ourselves do not wish to go there, it must be asked, how far do we remain south of it, or how near must we approach? Many of the gentlemen have taken post about the level of Kuttkulmen, but the ground there is quite open; the enemy can overlook our position in his advance from the east, he can advance east of Gumbinnen across the Rominte and

Pissa, and we must then deploy with the front towards the east. I think it would be best to remain about 4 miles from Gumbinnen and to place oneself in a position of readiness under cover behind the Plickner Berge.

But in taking up such an "alert position" one must always keep an eye on a position in which one will eventually defend oneself. Such a position cannot be exactly determined by the map, but must be selected on the ground. The General commanding sends with this object a General Staff Officer ahead, and himself rides there afterwards. The position behind the Plickner Berge seems to me at the same time favourable as a defensive position. The Cavalry can be placed under cover on the right wing ; the front has a clear field of fire, and the left wing is also leaning against the Angerapp, the less, it is true, the nearer we advance towards Gumbinnen. We now will have to send Horse Artillery under escort of Cavalry by the high-road against the enemy in order to gain touch of him. He will not leave us in possession of Gumbinnen ; he will drive away our Advanced Guard, which in its retreat towards the west can still take up an intermediate position. His Advanced Guard, which he doubtless will have formed, will then follow by Gumbinnen, and perhaps be still further strengthened from the Main Body.

The enemy now hears of our flanking position. He can then either retire again behind Gumbinnen with all his forces, or he can collect everything and attack us. The former, I daresay, he will not be able to carry out unmolested by us, as we assume the offensive, Cavalry ahead. In the other case we can remain for the present on the defensive. According to my opinion, owing to the improvements in firearms, the tactical defensive has gained a great advantage over the tactical offensive. We were always offensive, certainly, in the campaign of 1870, and attacked and captured the strongest positions of the enemy ; but, gentlemen, with what sacrifices ! It appears to me more favourable if the offensive is only assumed after repulsing several attacks of the enemy.

The question is now, whether we shall occupy Gumbinnen ? Those gentlemen who approached very close to it had to do so ; but I would not occupy Gumbinnen because I attach no value to its being passed by the enemy, and because I should more easily betray my intentions to the enemy.

Finally, I should like to add some further general remarks on the mode and manner in which some gentlemen have disposed of their Cavalry. The 1st Corps has a very strong Cavalry, 2 Divisions. All gentlemen have sent forward both against the enemy. We certainly had in 1870 also the mass of our Horse in front of the Army, but only so long as both Armies were still far distant from each other and when we were not yet acquainted with the enemy's position. But here, when we know where the enemy is, where both parties have approached each other to within some 28 miles, the Cavalry in front has no real object. ` It can only remain there halted or retire on the other bodies of the Corps. The Cavalry's place is behind the front at such a short distance from the enemy, and it will only be employed during the course of the battle, probably at the end of it.

I would try to gain touch of the enemy by the Cavalry on the high-road only, but send nothing south of it across the Rominte. A well-mounted officer suffices there. It is here not a question of delaying the enemy, but of only learning whether he is advancing, and in what direction. This an officer, who only relies upon his horse, will report to me just as well as a large mass of Cavalry. Besides, the enemy's attention would only be roused by its appearance on his left flank, which must be avoided.

In general, all gentlemen have worked intelligently, though they have not made use of all the advantages which the situation offered. They have proved that they understand how to lead mixed forces, which is after all the final aim of all our efforts.

SOLUTION OF THE 51ST PROBLEM.

A. *Written solution by General v. Moltke.*

I.

The leader of the Advanced Guard will hold the obstacle of the Fluth Graben, which in any case he can reach sooner than the enemy, and thereby procure time for the Corps to assemble.

But in order also to facilitate an offensive advance, if such be the intention of the General commanding, he will, as the next step, occupy Waltersdorf as well.

He sends orders to the Dragoon Regiment not to retire further than it is obliged, to observe the enemy, and to maintain Waltersdorf by dismounted Dragoons until relieved.

The 1st Battalion of Regiment No. 1 marches at once to Kieke-busch and occupies the village, the windmill, and the bridge.

The first 6-pr. Battery unlimbers to the left on the height 149 under escort of a Company of this Battalion.

· The 2nd Battalion turns off to the right through the nearest ride to Schulzendorf, and sends forward two Companies together with the Engineer Company to Waltersdorf, which is to be prepared for defence.

The 3rd Battalion, as a reserve, halts in the north corner of the Forst Wüstemark.

Report thereon to the General commanding, intelligence to the Advanced Guard of the 2nd Division.

2.

For the offensive as well as for the defensive solution of this problem the General commanding must first of all assemble his Corps.

He needs at least two hours to move up to the Advanced Guard behind the Fluth Graben with the leading troops of the columns of the Main Body. After the lapse of that time the enemy also may appear before this obstacle.

The 2nd Division receives orders to occupy with the Advanced Guard, Selchow and the bridges there, also to reconnoitre with its Cavalry the ground beyond Gr. Ziethen and Lichtenrade.

The Main Body of the Division marches by Rotzis to the Hohen Fichten. The 3 Batteries of the Division, accompanied by 2 Squadrons, trot ahead and take post west of the Fichten.

The 1st Division continues to advance by the high-road.

The General commanding goes himself to the height 149 at Kiekebusch, and eventually to the Marien Berg, where he can over-look the situation during the arrival of the columns.

If the enemy should already be advancing close to us with equal or superior strength his attack would have to be awaited.

The Infantry of the 2nd Division deploys to the left of the Fichten, and the position there can be strengthened by the calling up of Batteries of the Corps Artillery at an accelerated pace.

If there is still time for it, the 2nd Brigade of the 1st Division will advance by Waltersdorf and occupy the Marien Berg with 3 Battalions. From Selchow to Waltersdorf there is a front of about 4 miles.

If, however, the enemy has not advanced on his side, it may be concluded that he has not yet collected his forces. In order, now, to form an opinion on his strength, it becomes necessary to force him to deploy by approaching closer to him, and eventually to force him to retire.

The Battalions remain in column of route, use the existing bridges over the Fluth Graben, and only beyond it form up in mass of Brigades in line of columns of Regiments.

It is not probable that the enemy has squeezed himself into the ground between the line of lakes and the Spree ; we may presume him to be in the line, Rudow—Gr. Ziethen.

The Advanced Guard of the 2nd Division occupies Wassmannsdorf as a pivot for a left wheel of our front.

The leading Battalions of the 4th and 2nd Brigades extend in Company columns and send out skirmishers, and the Artillery moves into the alignment, Wassmannsdorf—Schönefeld—line of lakes. In any case, the enemy will now have to show his full strength and to decide for himself whether to accept battle or to retire.

If the attack is to be carried through on our part the Main Bodies of the 4th and the 2nd Brigades will follow, and the 3rd and the 1st form the reserve. The latter Brigade, in order to make sure of an eventual retreat, keeps the Marien Berg occupied.

The further measures will result from the course of the action.

The Trains remain behind the Notte bog.

B. *Verbatim shorthand report of General v. Moltke's verbal criticism.*

When considering a tactical problem one must in the first instance place oneself in the exact position of the enemy, and always assume him to adopt the most correct measures. The problem says, that hostile forces have collected in the neighbourhood of Eberswalde for the protection of Berlin. In what strength and how far the enemy has already advanced towards us is unknown. The straightest line for him is that by Cöpenick. If we advance in the direction of the capital we must encounter him.

So far, hostile troops which have advanced are ascertained : Infantry at Bohnsdorf, Artillery at Rudow, and Cavalry debouching at Glienicke. It may be presumed as likely that the enemy, in order to reconnoitre the ground to the south, has sent forward Cavalry, and, in order to secure its debouching, has already Infantry and Artillery standing in front of the defile. In no way would it be permissible to assume that the enemy stands in a position, Rudow—Bohnsdorf. This flanking position, with its rear towards the Müggel See and the swamp and wood defiles of the Spree, would be very disadvantageous. The enemy will also have tried to get on the roads by which we are advancing, and therefore positions Rudow—Buckow, or Rudow—Gr. Ziethen are more likely than one with its rear towards the Spree. If, therefore, the 2nd Division would advance on Rudow under the former supposition, it probably would not come in contact with the right wing, but with the left wing of the enemy, and get into a dangerous situation.

One more general remark I should like to advance. In order to make headway we need deep columns of route; but before an action we must close up. If we close up too early, we don't gain ground and are unnecessarily fatiguing our troops. If we close up too late the enemy can drive back the detachments covering us and attack us while we deploy. How, then, shall the closing up be carried out? There exists no rule for it; in each case that which is the most practical in the circumstances is to be done. But we have a medium still between the columns of route and the formed-up front: the marching of columns beside each other and a " position of readiness." Let us now turn to the problem itself, and first to the measures of the Commander of the Advanced Guard. Every Advanced Guard is to procure its Main Body time to prepare for action. It will be well if the Advanced Guard does so by making use of a favourable section of the ground for defensive action. Already from the map 1 : 100,000 it can be gathered that a pretty broad strip of meadow with ditches extends between Kiekebusch and Schulzendorf, offering advantages for defence.

The importance of Waltersdorf for a future offensive is evident, and this almost all gentlemen have recognised. An offensive on our part is not feasible if the enemy is in occupation of Waltersdorf. It only appears questionable whether we still reach that place before the enemy. If gentlemen send their Advanced Guard Battery thither, it may get into danger if a retreat by the Cavalry becomes necessary. The Commander of the Advanced Guard therefore would occupy the section Kiekebusch—Schulzendorf, and hold it under all circumstances, and next, if possible, take possession of Waltersdorf. The Advanced Guard has still an hour's march to Waltersdorf, and therefore a dismounted Squadron is to be charged for the present with its occupation until relieved by Infantry. The Commander of the Cavalry Regiment, I daresay, would in actual warfare do so on his own account; yet it does not seem to me superfluous to direct special attention to it. The rest of the Regiment would then have to stay in the neighbourhood, since part of it must always be ready to charge, if part is dismounted or holding horses. If this Cavalry is dislodged by Infantry the Dragoons certainly run as quickly as Infantry, but they can only be picked up if a part advances to charge the Infantry.

As regards the arrangements of the Commander of the Corps, he has a very difficult task; he does not know the strength of the enemy. It may happen to him as to the man who looked for the track of the lion and found the lion himself. He may find the enemy stronger than he thought. It is so easily said, to break off the fight and to retire behind the Notte bog, but it is difficult to withdraw the Corps from action, if part, perhaps a great part of it, is already engaged. For one must first get into column of route before one can march. In most cases it is better to carry through an action once begun, though it does not turn out favourably, than to break it off. Resistance must not be offered close in front of the defile; just as bad is it to occupy Mittenwalde and Königs-Wusterhausen; we weaken ourselves and are posted in the defile. The covering of a withdrawal can only be attained by a position lying far to the front of the defile. It results from this, that the General commanding has to take up a position in which he can accept the attack, from which he can assume the offensive, and into which he can retreat if the enemy is stronger. This position must be situated so that the enemy cannot reach it before us.

A position, Selchow—Kiekebusch, would fulfil these requirements; on the right wing it is already occupied by our Advanced Guard, and the Advanced Guard of the 2nd Division can soon reach Selchow. The difficulty of the obstacle in front cannot exactly be ascertained from the map 1 : 100,000, but in reality we have no better maps. It seems, at any rate, that the Fluth Graben can contribute to the strength of our defensive. The extent of the position is about four miles, an extent which an Army Corps may well embrace. The Corps will be deployed for attack on the line, Selchow—Kiekebusch if the enemy attacks or assembles for attack. When we speak of assembling we do not mean thereby the concentration at one point, but that the heads of columns are directed to a distinct point. The Advanced Guard of the 2nd Division at Selchow undertakes the securing of the left flank, the head of the Main Body would be directed by Rotzis to the patches of wood east of Selchow and there deploy to the left.

Whether on the arrival of the troops the position is to be taken up between Selchow and Kiekebusch or between Wassmannsdorf and the Marien Berg can only be decided on the spot after exact knowledge of it, and it further depends on the enemy's measures. The General commanding will himself go to the Advanced Guard of the 1st Division. His place during the action is in rear, but before the action the height at Kiekebusch (149) or the Marien Berg, if he can reach it, will offer him a good view for observing the enemy's measures and for forming his own resolutions. His columns, besides, have still a two hours' march to the position; it will therefore be taken up only between 1 and 2 o'clock. If the enemy is in the act of advancing, the Corps Artillery will be moved up at a trot; if the enemy is inactive, and therefore either too weak or not yet assembled, one's own advance is to be executed with great caution. It is not necessary to commence it with the former Advanced Guards, but these will hold Selchow and Waltersdorf occupied as pivots. The offensive movement is to be initiated from the centre by deploying only the heads of the columns, and is then to be continued by a left wheel. If we are on a level with Wassmannsdorf we will probably know what the enemy's intentions are.

SOLUTION OF THE 52ND PROBLEM.

Verbatim shorthand report of General v. Moltke's verbal criticism.

Some gentlemen have been doubtful from what hour the instruction to the General of Division is to be dated. I grant that the gentlemen would perhaps have seen it sooner if it were said in the problem " has . . . . given." But, surely, it might have been assumed that the General of Division must have had this instruction before he started on his march, which certainly should have begun at 9 o'clock even without instruction. But if he had received it only during his march, he could not have changed his order of march without loss of time and disorder. But the General commanding could also issue this instruction sooner, as he had already early in the morning

knowledge of the enemy's advance by Königs-Wusterhausen and Mittenwalde. For the appearance of hostile columns at Waltersdorf was immaterial to him ; at the utmost it gave him the certainty that the hostile columns were at that time still engaged in the defiles of the Notte, and that he therefore had still several hours' time before the enemy could get near his position. He further knew that about midday the 6th Division could arrive in support of him, and he could hope therefore to maintain himself in his position up to that time. Its left flank was less endangered than the right. In order to attack the former the enemy had to expose his own left flank and line of retreat. An attack of the enemy on the centre and right wing of the position at Gr. Ziethen was therefore more probable. His position was only about 2¼ miles long ; for the above reasons alone he would have concentrated his reserves behind the right wing. Now, could it be more desirable for him to move up to it also the Division from Tempelhof, or should he not have rather wished to employ it alongside in prolongation, or still better in advance of it?

He would have sent to the General of Division perhaps the following order : " I shall try to maintain myself in the position, Gr. Ziethen—Rudow. I count upon your being able to arrive in advance of my right flank about midday. If the enemy up to your arrival has not attacked I shall myself advance against him, and you at the same time have to form a right, advanced echelon of the 2nd Corps. While advancing in echelon you have to try by your offensive movements to drive the enemy from his line of retreat across the Notte defiles against the Spree."

This instruction had to suffice. The Divisional Commander is an old, experienced General, who can clearly discern his task from this brief instruction. It is a grateful one, for while the Corps was eventually undergoing a tedious frontal attack, his was the grateful task of attacking the left flank of the enemy with all the favourable results arising from the direction of such an attack.

Let us now turn to the General of Division. The 6th Division could march as far as Gr. Ziethen without being disturbed. Up to that point no enemy was in front, nor any on the flank. Still, in that direction it was necessary to reconnoitre towards Gr. Machnow. One to two Squadrons and some Officers' Patrols were sufficient for this. It is not necessary to send the whole Cavalry Regiment for this purpose, and it is disadvantageous to send the Cavalry Brigade. One must

not arouse the enemy's attention too early by deploying strong
Cavalry. For this reason I should not have patrolled further than this,
so as not to attract the enemy's attention to his left flank too early.
But as soon as the Division advances beyond the front of the 2nd
Corps it will have the enemy probably on its left flank. Therefore the
Division must assume an order of march which considerably departs
from that otherwise usual with us, and move so that by a simple " Left
turn " it can form up in battle order. In the first instance, the order
of march will differ from the usual one in that the Division does not
need an Advanced Guard, or if it forms one, in that it is closely followed by its Main Body.

Further, notwithstanding that the Division is marching to the
south, it will still engage the enemy first, towards the east. But we
form in two lines for action ; therefore the Division will march also in
two columns, in order to bring about by a simple " Halt, Front," the formation in two lines. Now, in both columns, we must in the first instance march with those arms which are first to come in contact with
the enemy. But Infantry and Artillery are needed first. In the left
column, therefore, will march the whole Artillery under protection of 3
Battalions at the head and again 3 Battalions in rear ; in the right
column, the other 6 Battalions followed by the Cavalry Brigade.
The latter we then can easily move up for action on this open ground
if wanted. Many gentlemen have attached this Brigade to the 2nd
Army Corps. I do not think this practical. Others have retained the
Brigade with the Division or placed it at the disposal of the General
commanding. But the Brigade is attached to the Division, and one
does not like to give away what is handed over to one. Besides, the
Commander of the Corps is at Gr. Ziethen, and cannot judge from
there when the moment has come for the action of the Cavalry
Brigade on the right wing ; the General of Division can judge better,
still better the General of Brigade himself. A third difference in the
order of march is that we do not march with a complete Brigade in
each column, but in both columns with a Regiment of each Brigade,
so that by a simple " Left turn," we can obtain the normal formation
for the single Brigades.

Some gentlemen have assigned to the Division a position of readiness. This requires a closing up at the least, and as the columns are
2½ to 3½ miles long, this forming-up would occupy more than one
hour. Besides, one does not know where this position of readiness

I

is to be taken up. If we form up at Lichtenrade and the enemy has not yet advanced beyond Selchow, we would have to get into column of route again for continuing the march, and thereby have lost two hours' time. Just as disadvantageous is it to order: "The Division will march to such-and-such a place, where it will await further orders." Gentlemen, in that case the General of Division does nothing at all. The orders which he was to be given could just as well have been sent to meet him on the march. Neither do I think it practical to let the left column march by Britz and Buckow. It there encounters first the Trains, then the reserves of the 2nd Corps south of Buckow, and then would either have to turn to Lichtenrade or to engage frontally at Gr. Ziethen.

I think it better to march with both columns on the high-road by Mariendorf—Lichtenrade, that is, to move the right column with a small detour by Lankwitz—Marienfelde, and thence over the open fields in the direction of the small bushes at Mahlow.

If we are marching then as indicated we form the order of battle by "Halt, Front." The Infantry wheels to the left, the wagons of the Artillery have to cover only 1,000 paces in order to reach their Batteries, and the second line places itself in proper order. Where this "Halt, Front," will take place depends upon the enemy. If he is standing already at Kl. Ziethen, the Artillery must unlimber east of Lichtenrade and the Division deploy for attack at that same place. If he were standing still at Wassmannsdorf or Selchow, one could have continued advancing ; if he were already retiring it would have been necessary first to occupy the heights of Gr. Kienitz with Infantry, in order then to move the Artillery up thither, and finally, if the enemy were still further back, one could have marched eventually as far as Gross or Klein Kienitz, in order to reach him on this side of the defile, where he was bound to lose time.

In war the measures depend on the circumstances as we find them. I believe that by these measures the greatest success can be obtained, though some of the different measures of several gentlemen would have also been fairly successful.

SOLUTION OF THE 53RD PROBLEM.

Verbatim shorthand report of General v. Moltke's verbal criticism.

Gentlemen, the problem had placed the Division for you in a somewhat difficult situation : March with exposed flank. Some of the gentlemen now have tried to improve the situation by letting the Division continue its march at once on the same evening. They will thus certainly reach Zehdenick safely ; but, gentlemen, you can do that only on paper, not in reality : there it would be quite different.

Others let the Trains start on the same night. Well, gentlemen, the troops want the Trains in the bivouac, and if you take these from them they simply become a hindrance. But if you still let them march in the evening, then go at once farther, at least as far as behind the Finow Canal, and not only into an intermediate position at Prenden. Others, again, have shifted the bivouacs in the evening, which, according to the problem, were round Biesenthal, to the west of that place. Gentlemen, imagine the situation as it is in reality. The Division only moved into bivouac in the evening, and therefore after a long march ; the kitchens are dug, the kettles on the fire. Then comes a General Staff Officer, and says: "The bivouac is to be shifted, you must move a little bit farther." Then the men must start again, the horses must be harnessed, the meat cannot be boiled; one does not do so in reality.

Some other gentlemen have made the situation still more difficult for themselves than that which the problem presented, and have assumed that the enemy is standing already at Basdorf and had already occupied the defiles of the Wandlitzer See and at Stolzenhagen. There are some even who imagine the enemy to be already at Zerpenschleuse. They said to themselves: "Since the enemy comes from Berlin, he can just as well march those 16 miles to Basdorf." Well, it is possible, but the problem says nothing about it. The enemy can certainly march with the Cavalry and Artillery and let the Infantry go by rail to Bernau, in order to keep it as fresh as possible.

I admit that the whole situation, so briefly stated, is somewhat improbable. A Prussian Division is marching from Frankfurt to Zehdenick while the enemy is at Berlin. But to state everything in the problem the whole history of a campaign would have to be given as an introduction. Not till then could one say: "That is possible and that is impossible."

I have taken the 5th Division because its composition is very simple and known to all. I could just as well have taken a Swedish or Russian Division, but then we had to work with troops unknown to us. Gentlemen had therefore to accept the situation simply as the problem stated it, and not to look for anything special beyond what is given, otherwise there is no limit to speculation. The enemy need not at all come from Berlin; he can also come from a greater distance. You therefore must not look behind the situation for a special trick, and think we wish to lay a trap for you.

We will now first ask ourselves, What can the enemy do? It is not probable that he will attack us at night. He must march through an extensive wood, and would then have made by the evening of the 1st September such preparations that he could not have taken so quietly our reconnaissances on Rüdnitz and Ladeburg. It is just as improbable that he will march the next day on Biesenthal; he would then march behind us and drive us, if circumstances were most favourable to him, in a direction where we wish to go. But if he were to march by the high-road from Berlin to Basdorf, he would make a great détour. If you measure it you will find that he has to cover about 4½ miles more. It is most probable, therefore, that he will advance in a straight line on Lanke or Forst Haus Liepnitz.

Now, almost all of the gentlemen have understood that the Division can no longer continue marching in its former direction by Lanke and make from there a turn by Klosterfelde, and almost all have therefore placed themselves on the road to Prenden. But they wanted to occupy simultaneously all the defiles as far as the Wandlitzer See, and thereby extended over 7 miles. That, however, is not at all necessary; one is perfectly in time, if one occupies one after the other of these defiles. Utzdorf and Lanke must, in any case, have been previously occupied.

The present Advanced Guard, however, can no longer reach the defiles on the high-road in time. At first it has a very unfavourable march through the wood. Already the march from Lanke to Utzdorf is difficult; one cannot march with a column of all arms north of the swampy meadows; one must therefore go round south of them. But one cannot give way there, and the Advanced Guard may get here into an unfavourable situation, if the enemy attacks from the south. Afterwards the Advanced Guard has to debouch from the wood at Forst Haus Liepnitz with a long column of route, and will hardly be able to form up in time and reach a defensive position behind the defiles at the Heilige Pfuhl. The Advanced Guard must remain therefore, and the defiles on the high-road must be secured by a special detachment from the direction of Klosterfelde.

Some gentlemen wished to await further reports first. But much time is then lost, and they still will get only reports that patrols met patrols. Precious time is lost before they know from where the enemy is coming.

One of the gentlemen has hit upon quite a different solution. This gentleman, while remaining with the Main Body on the high-road by Lanke, goes with the present Advanced Guard offensively against Ladeburg. It is right ; one can imagine every situation, defensively and offensively; but one does not know here the strength of the enemy, and has to make a march through a long wood defile. I have calculated on the particular paper the circumstances as they would arise if both parties started from Biesenthal and Bernau at the same time, and you will see that they are not favourable to us.

It seems to me the simplest and shortest way, if I read to you what I think the solution should be. It is advisable in such problems to draw up an order of march (*ad marginem*), so that it is at once seen from where the Regiments are taken.

1. ARRANGEMENTS FOR THE NIGHT.

Fusilier Battalion No. 8 (assumed by me as being with the Main Body) moves at once to the bridge over the Pfauen Fliess, posts pickets on the Langerönner Fliess, sentries at the edge of the wood. The 1st Squadron of Dragoon Regiment No. 12 goes back to Danewitz, patrolling during the night towards Ladeburg and Bernau. The roads from Biesenthal leading through the Stadt Heide to Marienwerder are to be reconnoitered at once. The Advanced Guard is informed of these arrangements, as well as of the intelligence received about the enemy. It pushes a Battalion out to the Vw. Utzdorf to-day, if possible, otherwise to-morrow very early ; it occupies the Hell Mühle and the bridges between the Hell lakes with Infantry, and causes Infantry to patrol towards the road Bernau—Basdorf. Lanke and Utzdorf are to be prepared for defence.

2. DISPOSITIONS FOR THE 2ND SEPTEMBER.

(The order of march is to be represented graphically *ad marginem*.)

H.Q. Biesenthal, 1st September, 8 p.m.

The Division continues its march to-morrow by Prenden, the

present Advanced Guard covering it as a Flank Guard. The Trains of the Division are assembled at 5 a.m. at the eastern exit of Biesenthal and march under escort of 1 Company of the Grenadier Regiment No. 8, and ½ a Troop of the 1st Squadron of the Dragoon Regiment No. 12, by Unter Försterei Eiserbude on Marienwerder, where they will find further orders.

A new Advanced Guard is formed by the Grenadier Regiment No. 12, the 2nd and 3rd Squadrons of Dragoon Regiment No. 12, and the 2nd Battery, who will march at 5 a.m. by Prenden to Klosterfelde. The Main Body follows immediately behind this Advanced Guard, but moves at Neudörfchen to the Prenzlau high-road at the Lottsche See, north of Klosterfelde.

At 7 a.m. the former Advanced Guard evacuates Lanke and Vw. Utzdorf and rejoins the Main Body by Prenden. The Division probably will be assembled at 9 o'clock on the Prenzlau high-road, and the newly-formed Advanced Guard (Regiment No 12) will from that moment form the Rear Guard to a further retreat, for which I shall issue the further orders on the spot.

3. EXPLANATIONS.

If the Main Body faces about on the Prenzlau high-road at the Lottsche See, it has its line of retreat on Berg and the Zerpenschleuse straight in its rear, and, accordingly, as the enemy follows by Lanke or Forsthaus, the 12th or 52nd Regiment* before it to cover further retreat. It can reinforce the one Regiment, or draw in the other, perhaps assume the offensive, according to circumstances, or retire at once behind the Finow Canal.

This, gentlemen, is only an example; in it I have given you only my opinions; this does not preclude others from being equally correct.

SOLUTION OF THE 54TH PROBLEM.

Verbatim shorthand report of General v. Moltke's verbal criticism.

The problem prescribed that the arrangements for the advance of the Division on Osterode were to be given; it is not meant by this that the enemy is to be attacked to-morrow as well. The distance to him is very great. Even if we assume our Advanced Guard to be in the neighbourhood of Platteinen, we have still 9 miles to the villages

---

* Assumed as the former Advanced Guard.

occupied by the enemy. It is therefore not wrong if we only advance to-morrow in order to attack him on the day after to-morrow. But, gentlemen, we have to consider at the same time that we will not gain the defiles, which are difficult to seize as they are, more easily on the next day; for if we delay the attack till after to-morrow the enemy will be able to adopt his counter measures as well for that day. It is therefore better if we carry out the attack on the same day (therefore to-morrow). Besides, the position in which we may suppose the enemy to stand is generally so strong that a frontal attack does not promise success, and that we must envelop the enemy, and therefore divide our forces. But it is impossible for us to bivouac for the night in two or three different bodies without exposing ourselves to the danger of being attacked by the enemy with superior force at one place.

Furthermore, it was said by some: The intelligence about the enemy is so scanty that I cannot yet form thereon a disposition for attack. That is indeed correct, but we need not base ourselves alone upon what we know, but may do so also on what we can assume as probable. Now, in order to learn more, many gentlemen have sent their whole Cavalry Brigade across the Grabitscheck. They will not learn more thereby than they know already. The Cavalry will also very soon encounter Infantry posts of the enemy there and not learn more. You can find out the same by single officers with some orderlies. But if we send the Cavalry across the Grabitscheck it is out of our hands.

I have previously mentioned that we could conclude with some probability where the enemy is to be found. He is standing in advance of Osterode, and here, as it were, in a square redoubt constructed by nature, with high parapets and wet ditches around. The key of this position, Hirschberg and Klein Gröben, he will have occupied with Infantry, having pushed forward two posts in order to hear of our advance; he then will deploy where that advance occurs.

Place yourself in the position of the enemy who is at Osterode. He will, at any rate, have occupied a position on the high-road to Hohenstein, that is, on both sides of the deep ravine at Warneinen. One could have reckoned on this in one's disposition. Now, the attack on this position will always remain difficult, but I have already mentioned that we would have to envelop the position, that is, we must divide our force. This we can also do, because we are superior. I have given you a normal Russian Division, while the enemy at Osterode has a Prussian Division. We thereby have a superiority of 4 Battalions, 4 Squadrons, and 14 guns. We can therefore divide ourselves, and it is only a question where we wish to advance for the main attack. We have three sections of ground here for an advance, which are defined by the deep ravines of the Grabitscheck and the Drewenz. If we advance on all three we have nowhere superiority, and risk an offensive by the enemy. We must therefore advance with one main column only. If we advance to the left of the Grabitscheck, which very many gentlemen have done, we separate ourselves from our own communications. And though one can effect one's retreat on Frogenau, to which place some gentlemen have directed their Trains, it is, after all, not altogether our line of retreat. That line was by Hohenstein, where most gentlemen have kept their Trains. Besides, we then have the enemy still in front in his exceedingly strong position, with the lake defiles and the deep valleys ahead of us.

Now, some gentlemen have marched across from Schildeck to Döhringen and left against Gross Gröben a few Battalions only, and often only Cavalry. But this march was only possible if Gross Gröben was taken. The attack on Gross Gröben is therefore the very first thing. Others went across the Grabitscheck, west of Reichenau. Gentlemen, that is a ticklish matter. Nothing at all prevents the enemy, when we are crossing the Grabitscheck, from advancing from Warneinen by Schildeck, and then he is between us. Besides, only two roads, and these, according to the map, not good ones (field-paths), lead from Reichenau over the Grabitscheck. I consider this the least favourable direction.

Some have advanced on the right bank of the Drewenz. Thereby one secures one's own communications best. One can attack Osterwein successively by Wittigwalde and Jugendfeld ; that will not be difficult; one will meet but little resistance. One can then by enveloping the position still further push on to Hirschberg, and from there to Lubainen. We thereby bring the enemy into a very disadvantageous situation, because he then leans with his rear against the row of lakes at Warneinen, and thus gives up Osterode.

But opposed to these advantages are also considerable objections. First of all we have for our advance only bad forest-paths, which mostly run in zigzag; it will be impossible to march in more than two columns. If we have taken Osterwein the ground very much narrows between the Osterweiner and Schilling lakes. There is no possibility of deploying our Artillery on that ground, while the enemy faces us on the heights at Hirschberg with strong Artillery on a broad front. Debouching from the wood at Bunken Mühle would be very difficult. You therefore see that by choosing this direction the advantages and disadvantages are pretty evenly balanced.

The same is the case with the third direction, if we advance by Reichenau. The Cavalry advances first of all, namely, before the Advanced Guard, and reconnoitres the ground as far as towards Gross Gröben. It will not be able to get any further in that direction, for we cannot expect it to attack Gross Gröben. Only the Advanced Guard can do that, and this it is able to do because it can attack and envelop the enemy. But in spite of this the further attack will still be very difficult, and only promise success if we oblige the enemy by demonstrations to detach a force from his position at Warneinen to Hirschberg. This can already be attained by weak forces. Not Regiments, or even Brigades, but only a few Battalions with some guns will be sufficient, because the enemy cannot discern our weakness in the close country in front of him, and does not know what may be hidden in the wood. But these troops must not then go beyond the wood, so as not to betray their weakness. This small detachment therefore is sufficient for demonstrating, and is besides so small that it can perhaps rejoin by the high-road by Osterwein, if the enemy drives it back. If we hold Gross Gröben, we can detach in the first instance Artillery under escort of Infantry from that place to Lichteinen, although not Cavalry. It will find there on the heights west of Lichteinen lake and at Lichteinen quite excellent positions. It can enfilade here the front of the enemy from Lichteinen to Warneinen, it facilitates the opening of the defile of Lichteinen by Infantry, which can then advance further from there. Nevertheless, the attack even in this manner has its difficulties, and we expose our own rearward communications as well. Both directions, therefore, have their advantages and disadvantages; we cannot say the one is wrong, the other is right. All we want is to see the measures properly carried out.

But of one thing I should still like to warn you, gentlemen, namely, not to say: " The troops are to wait for further orders." Such a measure paralyses the independent action of the subordinate leaders. The leader of the detachment, for instance, sees that he can easily take Osterwein, but he dare not ; or he sees that he can easily penetrate into Hirschberg simultaneously with the enemy, but he dare not because he is waiting for an order. The right moment is then easily missed. You must consider at the same time that you surely can send 'him without difficulty an order altering the former one. To detached leaders one must give only general instructions by which they can act freely. Such a measure is, however, quite useless for the Main Body of the troops, because the Commander. in-Chief will in most instances be present with that body.

It was further said : " I reserve to myself the further orders." Well, gentlemen, this is all very well in a disposition ; there one need not give any further explanations and reasons. You can hide your further intentions from your subordinate leaders, but in an examination question you must not withhold from us your further intentions, because you are to be judged by these. Well, gentlemen, I must unfortunately break off these exercises. I think, if we had still more time and could discuss some of the answers, we would very easily come to an understanding.

SOLUTION OF THE 55TH PROBLEM.

A. *Written solution by General v. Moltke.*

The Flank Detachment (31st Regiment, 1st and 2nd Squadrons Hussars No. 12 and 1 Battery) receives orders not to engage in an action, but, if the enemy advances as far as Schafstädt, to occupy the line Obhausen—Barnstädt, where the Detachment will be reinforced. A Company each will occupy Obhausen—Barnstädt, Nemsdorf, Göhrendorf; two Battalions, one Battery bivouac south of Grosse Mühle, Cavalry at Obhausen patrols against Schafstädt and Eichstädt. These troops form the Rear Guard.

Advanced Guard (71st Regiment, 3rd and 4th Squadrons Hussars No. 12 and 1 Battery) still occupies to-night the line Röblingen—Stedten, with 1 Company each ; 2½ Battalions bivouac on the height near Laura Schacht, Cavalry in Schraplau, reconnoitres towards Steuden.

Both bodies of troops maintain connection and observe the ravine.

16th Brigade : 96th Regiment alarm quarters, Querfurt.

   72nd   „   „   Lodersleben,
Döcklitz and
Gatterstedt,
Artillery and 5th Squadron 12th Hussar Regiment
at Farnstedt.

For to-morrow : The Division continues its march on Eisleben. The 16th Brigade, rendezvous 6 o'clock, north of Döcklitz. In case the enemy advances sooner against Querfurt, the Rear Guard, maintaining Obhausen and occupying Querfurt, withdraws behind the valley between these places. Should the Rear Guard be severely pressed, the Main Body of the Division will take up a position on the heights behind Hornburg, the Advance Guard joining it behind Erdeborn.

Trains early by Wolferstedt and Bornstedt to Eisleben.

B. *Verbatim shorthand report of General v. Moltke's verbal criticism.*

Some gentlemen have rendered the problem more easy for themselves by marching beyond Querfurt. One could, perhaps, under present circumstances consider it advisable to make a very long march : occasionally that is the only safeguard. I remind you of the Corps Vinoy which marched day and night, and could only thus escape to Paris. But in what state did it arrive there! Here, there was no necessity for making a forced march. We had 14 miles to Querfurt, and that is for a Division marching on one road a sufficiently long march. Querfurt offers an opportunity for sheltering the troops well ; bivouacking at the beginning of March is no pleasure, and particularly harmful to horses. Moreover, it was distinctly stated in the problem that the Division was to march from Freiburg to Querfurt on the 1st March.

Other gentlemen bring in an arbitrary condition by counting upon reinforcements. But nothing was said of this in the problem. They count upon the support of the 7th Division, and together with it want to assume the offensive. But they did not know at all whether the Division had already arrived at Eisleben. I also find fault with the moving up of an ammunition column. That measure points to an intention to court a decisive battle, and yet it ought to be your endeavour to get away if possible without any fighting. You ought to have been glad of having your Trains so far away.

The enemy at midday had been seen advancing from Merseburg

on Lauchstädt and Clobicau. You do not know much about him. Nevertheless it is not possible to say : " I shall await further reports before I form further resolutions." I have already on a former occasion spoken against ordering troops to march to there and there and to await there further orders. By such an order you cause that nothing at all is done. One must give a distinct order for acting, and can, in case of necessity, send an altered order afterwards. Whether, now, the enemy halts to-day at Lauchstädt—Clobicau and only with the Advanced Guard goes forward to Schafstädt—Eichstädt or on Steuden, or whether he marches still further, you cannot know. It is not probable, but it is possible, and you must at any rate secure yourself against it.

If the enemy does not attack on the 1st March, his attack on the 2nd is not to be expected in the direction of Querfurt, but in that of Stedten. In the former direction he would attain nothing but the retirement of your Rear Guard, and, that, just to the place whither it is your intention that it should retire. The enemy would therefore march behind you.

The enemy's attack is to be expected with certainty on the 2nd March. We would therefore secure the ground here by a well-timed defence of this section which is so advantageous. In doing so we could adopt two modes, both of which I consider correct. Either the Flank Guard gives way on Stedten and the covering at Obhausen is to be undertaken by the Advanced Guard of the Division, which at Göritz turns off to that place,—or the Flank Guard retires to Obhausen and the Division pushes out a Detachment (Advanced Guard) by Querfurt to Schraplau and Stedten.

I prefer the second solution because it is the simplest. But at any rate it is necessary that the Detachment, which is sent to Schraplau, receives the peremptory order to occupy the section of the ground there and to hold it. Some papers contain a solution, which is a very near approach to the correct one, but the order for each Detachment is not clearly expressed. Other papers miss the point, but are worded so precisely and clearly that one must say the writer is well able to solve another problem correctly.

Where several of the papers have adopted the half measure of letting the Detachment designated for Stedten march on the 1st March only as far as Döcklitz or Schafsee, they have thereby implied the apprehension that the whole distance might be too far. I think that in the present instance the distant march was justifiable and could very well be executed by the Detachment ; a Regiment marches its 18 miles much more easily than a whole Division.

As regards now the further advance of the Division on the 2nd March, I should like to pronounce against a start during the night. By an early start merely there is no security attainable, for the enemy can start on his march just as early as we can. I am especially against a night march of the Trains ; they are really safe enough already owing to their distance.

By which road now is the Division to march? Very many gentlemen started by the high-road ; it certainly is the safest road. But if the Division marches there, you surely place your Detachment at Stedten in a very serious position. Either it has to give way before hostile superiority, and then you are very soon disturbed in your advance (for if the enemy approaches only to within $2\frac{1}{2}$ miles you must get off the road and at least partly deploy against him),—or you expose your Detachment to annihilation, if it has to hold on (for the distance from Rothen and Schirmbach is too great for an eventual support). I would march in two columns by Alberstädt and Hornburg; a timely support of the Detachment is then ensured

SOLUTION OF THE 56TH PROBLEM.

Missing.

SOLUTION OF THE 57TH PROBLEM.

A. *Written solution by General v. Moltke.*

I.

The General Commanding will accomplish his task best by occupying a position in advance of the railway line which is to be protected. He thus gains in his front the strong obstacle of the Seille, secures, later on, his retreat on Metz, and at any rate prolongs the time which the enemy needs to reach the railway.

There is every probability that the enemy will use the permanent bridge over the Mosel at Pont-à-Mousson, which he is in possession of, and the roads leading therefrom. This determines the direction for the advance of the Main Body of the Division.

The necessity, however, of covering the right flank makes the sending of strong Detachments to the lower Seille unavoidable.

Whether it will be possible as the next step to advance as far as the Mosel cannot at this moment be determined.

2.

Since the Seille is still in our possession, the Division, after a fatiguing railway journey, may be granted the benefit of billets in cantonments in advance of Courcelles as far as Mécleuves and Silly; the advance from there can also be made in separate columns of route.

At daybreak at 5 o'clock on the 2nd May the 1st Infantry Brigade, the 1st Squadron of Hussars, the 1st and 2nd Batteries assemble at Mécleuves.

The 1st Battalion of the 1st Regiment, together with the 1st Battery, march straight to Pouilly and put Marly in a state of defence with one Company, destroying the bridge there. The Battery will take up a position, according to the probable enterprises of the enemy, on the height 203 west of or eventually south of Pouilly, whence the flat and open ground is commanded from Augny as far as Coin.

The Main Body of the Brigade marches by Orny and Verny as far as Louvigny, but leaves the 2nd Battalion of the 1st Regiment, together with the 2nd Battery at Verny, and occupies both the Bois de Lamencé and Pommérieux with one Company. The bridge leading to Coin is to be destroyed, that to Sillegny as well, and to be swept by fire from the Battery close to and east of Pommérieux.

The Cavalry Brigade, which withdraws its patrols from the other bank of the Seille and posts a line of relais on the road Pouilly— Louvigny, moves from Verny to Vigny, and places itself under cover in the valley south-west of the latter place.

The 2nd Infantry Brigade, the 2nd, 3rd, and 4th Squadrons of Hussars, the 3rd and 4th Batteries also, assemble at 5 o'clock at Silly, and advance by Vigny towards Louvigny.

The 10 Battalions, 19 Squadrons, and 3 Batteries, which are assembled here, occupy a position on the height 253 in advance of the road Verny—Raucourt. Louvigny and St. Jure on both wings will be occupied. A Detachment at la Hautonnerie destroys and watches the bridge at Moulin Neuf. Only a post of observation will be sent forward to Cheminot, which can be enveloped on all sides.

In front of the position of Louvigny, in which the attack of the enemy can be awaited, shelter-trenches are to be dug at once, giving cover to the men lying down without appreciably hampering an offensive advance even of Cavalry.

Gun-emplacements are to be constructed for the Artillery at the points most suitable, the Batteries, however, remaining at disposal in rear until a hostile attack has declared itself.

The permanent bridges at Longeville and Les Menils being in any case not easily destroyed, are only to be barricaded, because the attack from there is desired, and also in order to preserve the possibility of an advance against the Mosel.

B. *Verbatim shorthand report of General v. Moltke's verbal criticism.*

It was our task to cover the most exposed part of the Metz—Saarbrücken railway, the part from Courcelles to Han, against extensive enterprises of the enemy, probably because still further transport was to be conducted into Metz. It is certainly clear that in order to solve this problem we must occupy a position in advance of the railway concerned. Imagine, gentlemen, that we could, for instance, execute six marches more towards the enemy, we would then be in a position to keep him off the railway for five days without fighting, and during that time several Army-Corps could have been sent off.

Here the circumstances are not so favourable, as the Division is to complete the garrison of Metz later on. An offensive against the Mosel is thus precluded from the outset. We must rather act, therefore, on the defensive, and make use here of the features of the ground. Since we can execute only a single march without encountering the enemy, we must try to reach the Seille on the 2nd May; at what point of the stream we shall decide later on.

In the papers of the gentlemen three kinds of solutions are distinctly discernible. To begin with, several of you have advanced to Buchy or its neighbourhood (Solgne, Luppy). But there you find no support at all from the ground; you can be outflanked and driven away from the railway, as well as from Metz. That fortress not only lies on the flank of your position, but even in advance of the prolongation of the front of the Division.

Some gentlemen for that reason do not intend to remain at Buchy; they wish to await further reports, and then to advance against the enemy. But till to-morrow morning you will not get any further reports about the enemy, and what was heard about him to-day, that you know already. To-morrow you can, in addition, learn at the most that the Cavalry patrols received just the same Infantry fire from Nomény, whither the enemy meanwhile has advanced, as they received from the heights on the Mosel on the 1st of May. If you then march against the enemy you can no longer prevent his debouching, and must perhaps fight on quite unfavourable ground ; for you do not exactly know where you will encounter him.

Those gentlemen who wish to await further events at Buchy do not fulfil the demands made upon them. They express, thereby, that the General Idea, which was given to them, is incomplete, and that they expect a new one. Some gentlemen have moved into a flanking position at Verney. Something may be said in its favour, but there are also objections to it ; for that position does not quite fulfil one of the most important requirements of a flanking position, namely, that we can act upon the enemy's line of retreat. While we base ourselves upon the single point, Metz, the enemy has a much greater choice—he can retire everywhere on the wide arc of Pont-à-Mousson by Nomény, and still further to the east. If, for instance, he has crossed at Cheminot, and then has to face towards Verny, he has Nomény in his rear.

The destruction of the bridges, with the object of securing the right flank, I consider practical, because for an eventual vigorous offensive one surely sticks to the high-roads. But, at any rate, something besides must be done for securing the rear, as otherwise the enemy can make us very uneasy by demonstrating on the Lower Seille whilst crossing at the Upper Seille.

I would have detached a Battalion with a Battery to Pouilly. The Battalion would have occupied both Pouilly and Marly with 1 Company, while the Battery commanded the whole country at Cuvry and Coin from the height east of Marly. The enemy cannot then attempt bridging operations at that place.

With the Main Body I would have marched to Louvigny. If, in that case, we detach another Battalion with another Battery to Verny, the Lower Seille is completely secured. If the enemy then crosses at Cheminot, which is the most favourable point for him, he cannot comfortably deploy on the narrow strip of country east of that place, while we meet him on a broad front. If he advances from Nomény we can just as well meet him at Louvigny. I therefore consider a position at Buchy as faulty, and an advance from there as of doubtful success. A flanking position at Verny can perhaps attain good results, but I myself would have gone to Louvigny.

Those gentlemen who were of a different opinion have developed their views often very clearly and distinctly, although they arrived at different results. I willingly grant that the problem was difficult. One thing more I should like to notice : Many gentlemen, and particularly those who are mounted, have not used their Cavalry properly. They order it to "maintain" the Seille line. I think that is demanding too much ; this the Cavalry cannot be asked to do. It always feels uncomfortable on foot, and I think it is more easy to attack a village with dismounted men than to defend it. The garrison of a village does not know what is going on outside—it is afraid of the led horses being moved away, etc.

SOLUTION OF THE 58TH PROBLEM.

A. *Written solution by General v. Moltke.*

The high ground at Louvigny offers, also with the front to the south, a position with a clear field of fire in front and dominating the opposite slopes, in which the Division has its line of communications with Metz perpendicular in its rear. The enemy has his communications on the flank, and cannot march past our position without laying them entirely open.

After the attack on the Lower Seille has been repulsed and after the enemy's departure from there, it will be admissible to charge the 1st Battalion of the 1st Regiment and the Battery alone with the guarding of the stream upwards as far as Pommérieux, and to draw in the 2nd Battalion and Battery No. 2 from Verny to Louvigny the same night.

I.

The Division faces south and awaits the attack of the enemy.

The existing field work on the height 253 serves as a pivot for the right wing. The crest of the valley of the Vigny brook will the same night (otherwise to-morrow morning) be provided with shelter-trenches and gun-emplacements. St. Jure and Allémont, lying within the most effective fire of our Artillery, will be occupied and put in a state of defence. After occupying the shelter-trenches the Infantry posts itself for the present under complete cover of the reverse slope of the heights, the Cavalry behind Vigny, whence it threatens the enemy's advance on his right flank.

K

The distance from Louvigny to Vigny is too great for completely occupying it with one Division. Both villages, however, receive a small Infantry garrison, and one or the other may be reinforced according to the progress of the fight.

2.

The Division attacks the enemy opposing it.

The enemy has retained posts at Longeville and Les Menils. The Detachment at Marieulles has to march 3 to 4 hours if it wishes to unite with its Main Body at Raucourt. If the enemy weakens himself there by advancing with strong Detachments against the railway (small ones our Cavalry will prevent) we are superior in numbers when acting offensively, and there is a probability of beating the enemy at Raucourt before the arrival of his reinforcements from Marieulles.

Under cover of our Artillery the Battalions cross the Vigny brook ; with St. Jure, eventually Allémont, as a pivot, they form in two lines on the left bank. The Cavalry advances at a trot by the high-road towards Louvigny, crosses the brook at Moulin de Moince, and places itself on the right wing of the Infantry, where it will find the best ground for charging, threatening at the same time the enemy's retreat. Two Batteries thereupon follow the movements of the Infantry and direct their fire at short ranges against Raucourt and the salient of the wood of Ressaincourt.

The enemy will have to recall his Detachments from Secourt with the utmost speed to Mailly, but probably be already defeated at Raucourt.

This offensive movement would be in that case no longer possible should the troops from Marieulles have previously joined at Raucourt. Even a defence on the heights of Louvigny appears no longer advisable if these troops have already reached Cheminot.

3.

The Division retires on Verny. It is reinforced by the 1st Battalion and the 1st Battery.

The retirement is made by four parallel roads between Pommérieux and Liéhon, screened by the high ridge of Louvigny, with the Battalions first, then with the Artillery in echelon, finally with the firing line and the Cavalry flanking it.

The height between Verny and Cherisey affords to a force like the Division a position with a clear field of fire ; to the right the Bois d'Avigy to be occupied. Reserves screened.

The enemy will hardly dare continue marching in an easterly direction without attacking the Division standing at the same moment on his left flank at a distance of only 2½ miles.

The position at Verny can only be enveloped on its left wing where Orny and Bois des Veaux then afford fresh pivots to the defender. The assailant has also to make ample provision for securing his own lines of communication.

Against a decisive superiority the Division can no longer carry out both tasks, but only one of them, the reinforcing of Metz. But after having gained 5 to 6 days the covering of the railway is perhaps no longer necessary, or is undertaken by other troops.

B. *Verbatim shorthand report of General v. Moltke's verbal criticism.*

On the evening of the 3rd May we are well acquainted with the state of affairs on the enemy's side. There is no reason for assuming that after to-day's vain attempts to cross the stream at Verny— Marly he will again advance to-morrow against the lower Seille. We can therefore draw in the Verny Detachment to the Division and the Pouilly Detachment to Verny. I think we can even order the Battery of the latter to come up, which, for greater security, perhaps, would leave a few guns at Pommérieux. All these movements would of course have to be executed in the evening of the 3rd, and this by way of Goin, in order to remain unnoticed by the enemy.

The enemy is opposed to us in two separate groups ; the situation of the Reserve Division is therefore clear. Now, most gentlemen have said that, in case the enemy attacks to-morrow from the direction of Raucourt, they will remain at Louvigny. I assume they do not mean to imply to-day's position, for that was facing towards the west, and would therefore present its left flank to the enemy. Now, I should have liked those gentlemen to furnish a description of the position facing south, for surely one must be clear beforehand how one wishes to use one's troops. Some gentlemen wish to transfer their left wing to Allémont. But this has the disadvantage of being commanded by the height west of the Bois de Ressaincourt and of dividing the position into two parts by the Vigny brook, which renders the movements of troops very difficult. I would have posted myself on the line Louvigny—Vigny, where I start from the supposition that the troops are bivoucking along the road connecting those places

with outposts pushed towards St. Jure and Cheminot. But the position Louvigny—Vigny is 4,000 paces long, and that is too much for a Division. The right wing will have to be formed therefore by a Battery on the height 253 (south of Louvigny), which may be there already as a result of yesterday's entrenching. It flanks the ravines of the Vigny brook and of the Seille. A second Battery would have to be constructed about 2,500 paces east of Louvigny as a support for the left flank; in addition to this a slight shelter-trench is to be excavated along the crest of the valley so that our skirmishers can easily sweep the bottom. Allémont, St. Jure and Moulin de Moince are to be occupied by advanced posts. The two former places would have to be obstinately defended, as they are within effective range of our Artillery; the Mill, however, is to be occupied only slightly, for there are 6 to 8 crossings. Generally, such a brook is not a real obstacle at all. At Wörth we went through a very different kind of water. Also to Louvigny and Vigny I would detach only a few troops, but should circumstances afterwards demand it I can always reinforce the garrison there. The Cavalry is standing screened behind Vigny, the Reserves behind the left wing, for that is refused; and the greatest danger for us is to be pushed against the Seille and to be driven away from Metz.

On this occasion I must refer to some of the papers, the writers of which have in an independent clear exposition decided in favour of the offensive. Therewith they settle indeed all three possibilities,— that is to say, if they are victorious. But, surely, that is very doubtful, for if we ourselves attack we transfer all advantages of the defence to an equally strong opponent. We must attack frontally, and that surely would be very unsafe, for experiences of the last war teach us that the attacking party only succeeded when enveloping one wing. But to do so a superiority is wanted which we do not possess. Our attack will be brought about quite naturally if the enemy commits the blunder of detaching a force against the railway, and of consequently weakening himself before he has defeated the Division. If he detaches a weak force he will not get to the railway at all; if he detaches a strong one we beat the part left behind the more easily, and the rest retreats as a matter of course.

The mode of attack may vary much, as is always the case with such things. In illustration I will mention here only one such case, namely, a right wheel of the Division while maintaining St. Jure

The close country there I like much better for the decisive arm than the open ground further west. I first concentrate my Artillery fire on the Bois de Ressaincourt, and then have it stormed by an Infantry Regiment from Allémont. The possession of this wood has a two-fold value. Firstly, I can collect behind it everything, and from there easily take possession of the village of Ressaincourt. Secondly, the wood affords to me a pivot against the hostile Detachment returning from the east. After gaining the line St. Jure—Ressaincourt, the Division advances to attack the main position at Raucourt. The Cavalry finds employment partly on the left wing in reconnoitring towards the east, partly it has to act on the right wing on the open ground towards Eply. This is only one example; there are many possibilities.

Some gentlemen follow the enemy by Buchy. But the enemy has a start; he can have occupied the height in the neighbourhood of that place at least with a Detachment before we have come up. The Division must then either attack this strong position or remain halted at Vigny. But it can get there into an awkward position; if the enemy advances from Buchy and Raucourt it must then go back to Verny. Finally, on the departure of the Division to Buchy, a Rear Guard, which is left behind at Louvigny in order to cover this flank-ing movement, may, in case it does not follow quickly enough, be driven away from its Main Body by the enemy coming from Rau-court.

As regards the third case, some gentlemen say that they remain at Louvigny until they have forced the enemy to deploy. But that is not at all necessary, for the enemy will deploy of his own accord. We cannot control the departure of the party from Marieulles, but certainly the arrival of that column. If the enemy advances on Cheminot, it is high time to retire, for the covering of the railway must give way here to the safe retreat on Metz.

The Division had to go back in the first instance as far as Verny. If the Rear Guard, which must remain at Louvigny only up to the moment at which the enemy advances from Cheminot or St. Jure, should be pressed, detachments could then occupy the Bois de la Hautonnerie for the Rear Guard to fall back upon. But it is not right to make the whole Division go only as far as Hautonnerie.

According to the map the position at Verny is moreover not bad, the right wing is covered by the Seille, a possible still further retreat is also favoured by the woods situated in the north. Those parts of the enemy which started from Marieulles will have already marched more than 9 miles when they arrive before Verny, which is also not quite unimportant.

This is nearly all that I have to say in reference to these papers. If one wishes to answer such questions as are set here, one likes to look for certain rules and axioms. Such can, however, be only offered by science, and that, in our case, is strategy. But strategy is not of a kind like the abstract sciences. These have their invariable and precise truths upon which we can build, and from which we can draw further conclusions. The square on the hypotenuse is always equal to the sum of the squares described on the sides which contain the right angle; that remains always true, be the right-angled triangle large or small, be its vertex turned to the east or the west.

Now, we read much in theoretical books about the advantages of "operating on the inner lines." In spite of that we must still ask ourselves in each case what at the moment is the most advantageous. In our last problem we were standing also on the inner line, and knew the enemy's weakness at Marieulles, yet to none of the gentlemen did it occur to advance across the Seille against Marieulles.

Strategy is the application of common sense to the conduct of war. The difficulty lies in its execution, for we are dependent on an infinite number of factors, like wind and weather, fogs, wrong reports, etc. If, therefore, theoretical science alone will never lead us to victory we must nevertheless not entirely disregard it. General v. Willisen very truly says : " It is only a step from knowing to doing but it is a still greater from not knowing to doing." The best lessons for the future we draw from our own experience ; but as that must always be limited we must make use of the experience of others by studying military history. Besides which, another means of further ing our education is the working out of such supposed warlike situa tions as our problems present.

SOLUTION OF THE 59TH PROBLEM.

A. Written solution by General v. Moltke.

The enemy advancing from Frankfurt may have the intention either of directly joining by two marches from Kerstenhausen the defeated Corps about Wolfhagen, or of disengaging it by advancing against the left flank of the pursuers.

In the former case he will take the road by Fritzlar—Lohne, in the latter by Dorla and by Nieder Vorschütz. To occupy the three points mentioned would scatter the forces of the division; it is advis-able to keep it collected for the present at Gudensberg until the advance of the enemy can be ascertained.

For that purpose the Cavalry, with some Horse Artillery guns, is to be pushed out towards Fritzlar, Ober and Nieder Möllrich; Infantry posts in support of them at Werkel, Ober, and Nieder Vorschütz.

If the enemy crosses the Eder at Nieder Möllrich with his Main Body, a position can immediately be taken up towards Nieder Vor-schütz. Right wing occupying Ober Vorschütz strongly, left wing Maderstein and Landen Berg weakly, reserve behind Maderstein, Artillery on the Maderholzfeld.

If the enemy advances by Fritzlar, a position is to be occupied at Dorla : Artillery on both sides of the village commands the approaches to Werkel and Wehren, as also the lowlands of the Ems. Ober Vorschütz will be sufficiently occupied by Infantry. The Main Body of the Division stands perfectly covered from view behind the Nacken, and can support the one or the other wing as required.

If the enemy takes the road by Lohne, he cannot pass the Division, as he is still within effective range of our guns; he would have to attack the steep heights of the Weissenborner Feld across the Ems.

B. *Verbatim shorthand report of General v. Moltke's verbal criticism.*

We will place ourselves at once in the position of the Corps advancing from the south. It appears that it was meant to advance as a reinforcement for the Western Corps. Meanwhile the latter has suffered a defeat, and is pushed back. Now, what can the Southern party do ? Two things : It can advance either by the road north-ward in direct support of its defeated countrymen, or it can continue its march on Cassel, and aid them indirectly by threatening our own line of communication. As regards the former, it is doubtful whether this Southern Detachment will find the Western Corps still at Arol-sen ; where, and whether at all, cannot be foreseen. It depends on the condition of the Western troops and the energy of the pursuit.

Perhaps the other means lead to the goal more surely : threaten-ing the hostile communications by an advance on Cassel. But the party advancing from the south now learns that a Division of the enemy has meanwhile advanced south of Cassel. That Division is exceedingly awkward for it; the Division can move against its flank when it is marching towards the north, or oppose it frontally when advancing towards Cassel. It is in the interest of the Southern Detachment to attack the Division on the morning of the 3rd May, and from this I conclude that we, the 22nd Division, are justified in waiting and permitting an attack on us, if that is in our interest.

I think that some gentlemen have attached too great value to the apprehension that the enemy could march past us, and too little value to the preservation of their communications. If two bodies have approached to within a distance of one day's march, they would in reality *not* march past each other. On the other hand, one's own line of communication is an exceedingly ticklish thing. We had such a case, as you may remember, in the last war. Before Metz, we were standing on the 18th of August with the front facing east, but, mark you, after we had gained a battle two days previously. Up to that time we had wisely enough left the 1st Army on the east side for the protection of our communications. Still more dangerous was the situation in January, 1871, in the south-east of France. The greatest crisis would have occurred if General v. Werder had been beaten there by Bourbaki, and if the latter had advanced on our communications in a northerly direction. We would have been obliged to form quite a new Army in order to prevent all that.

Now, if we were equal to the enemy or stronger than he, we could do nothing better than to advance on Fritzlar, in order to accept the final issue on the open field there between Ems and Eder; we thereby would prevent his advance towards Arolsen and Cassel. But since we know that we are weaker, considerably weaker, we must look round whether the ground offers compensation for our numerical weakness. Then the line of the Ems presents itself to us, and we can reach it in any case before the enemy. It offers us a succession of good positions, for the northern bank almost throughout commands the southern, and in each of the positions we have excellent pivots and a clear field of fire. Our great want is to know where we are to stand on the Ems, for the whole arc—Kirchberg to Böddiger—we cannot occupy in a proper tactical manner.

Most gentlemen have also said very correctly : " At Holzhausen we cannot remain, we must advance further. We will take up a position of readiness at Gudensberg ; anything beyond that measure must then depend on those of the enemy." Whether at Gudensberg, south-west of Gudensberg, at the Nacken, or at the Wein Berg, is nearly all the same. Gudensberg lies in the centre of the arc which the Ems here describes. For that reason you were not asked in the problem for a Divisional order; there could be nothing else stated in it but a simple order of march of the Division. All the rest must be reserved, for we do not know what is going to happen.

It, further, is a general rule in war that a body of troops does not march without an Advanced Guard; but in war it is always a question of adopting for each particular case what is the most practical without adhering to unvarying general rules. Here we wish to take up a position of readiness from which to change at once into the fighting position. Now, several gentlemen have formed strong Advanced Guards: 3 Battalions, several Squadrons, 1 Battery, and then became embarrassed as what to do with them. They sent them to Dorla, and that is intrinsically a judicious direction; for it is most likely that the enemy will advance by Werkel. But what if the enemy came after all by Nieder Vorschütz and we were attacked there? We would then miss a good part of our forces; they would have to be called in first. It is therefore essential to keep the forces together. What afterwards should be done from the direction of Gudensberg some gentlemen have tried to elaborate in an abstract manner on generally perfectly correct theoretical grounds, and have overlooked thereby that it is a question of finding out what the enemy could do on the 3rd May, what intentions he could carry into execution. We can find it out only by our Cavalry. Certainly, most gentlemen said " We must reconnoitre; we send forward officers and patrols." But, gentlemen, these meet hostile patrols, and if the latter are stronger, they must go back, and are prevented from seeing. The Cavalry, it is true, is not to fight battles; it is only to see, yet I believe it was advisable to push out the whole Uhlan Regiment. The enemy evidently must cross one of the bridges of the Eder, either at Fritzlar or at Nieder Möllrich. I would send, therefore, 1 Squadron towards Fritzlar, ½ a Squadron towards both Ober and Nieder Möllrich, and would keep 2 Squadrons in reserve. Surely, the enemy would have to be advancing in great force, if our Cavalry could not have an opportunity of watching his movements beyond the Eder. We cannot go beyond the Eder, as it will be occupied; but I believe that such a strong force of Cavalry can remain on the northern bank of the Eder until clouds of dust or the heads of columns of the advancing enemy become visible. If the enemy is marching by Fritzlar or Nieder Möllrich we know whether to advance to Dorla or to Maden.

If you look at the map in these two main directions you will find that we have everywhere very good positions. At Maden we can post the Reserves behind the village or at the Maderstein, Artillery pushed out on the Maderholzfeld, to the right Ober Vorschütz strongly occupied, to the left the Itters Berg,—that is a strong position. But if the enemy should wish to envelop our left flank, we find a new position further to the rear. The three bridges (Werkel, Ober, and Nieder Vorschütz) must certainly be occupied, but only with weak Infantry Detachments, not Battalions ; that enables the Cavalry to remain longer in advance, and to observe more securely. At Dorla there is also a good position. Werkel, situated in advance of the salient, we certainly cannot maintain to the end. At last, also, the Artillery positions on the Mühlenberg would have to be evacuated if the enemy advances from the direction of Wehren, but at the beginning it would have a fine effect on the enemy's advance. We then would find behind Dorla a second position with pivots for the wings on both sides, and we retain our line of retreat straight in our rear.

It still remains to be settled what would happen if the enemy marches away to the north. Some gentlemen want to go across the Ems in order to attack him, or to march by Kirchberg or Wichdorf—Merxhausen, in order to take up a position in the valley of the upper Ems. This I would not advise in any circumstances. There is no position in the valley of the upper Ems, no obstacle is found there in front, and if the enemy leaves opposed to our front an equally strong force he can envelop our right flank with his overplus, and drive us against the defiles of the Ems, which just there are very difficult. We certainly have then, in the most favourable case, our retreat still on our 21st Division ; but if we arrive defeated not much good is gained. On the other hand, since the enemy will attack us in all circumstances, we find, in case of his advance to the north, a good position between Kirchberg and Dorla.

Therefore, a position of readiness at Gudensberg, such as was taken up by most gentlemen,—but then : reconnaissance of what the enemy is carrying out on the morning of the next day, and accordingly adoption of the further measures—that appears to me the correct solution of the question. I grant, the problem was difficult, because we know so little of what the enemy is doing; but so it happens to the weaker side in war as a rule.

You will get one more problem which is simpler, and you will work it out simply also, and not bring in things which lie outside of it. If gentlemen have puzzled their heads as to whether the 12th and 13th Army Corps are following behind the 11th Army Corps, if they ask: What will happen if the enemy makes a left turn at Kerstenhausen in order to unite with the Western Corps somewhere in Westphalia, or if he advances on Cassel on the right bank of the Fulda?—well, gentlemen, these are quite new problems, and all the military, strategical, and political circumstances would have to be presented to you. You must confine yourselves to what is given.

In conclusion, I wish further to remark that a logical development of the idea, a correct and clear manner of writing, and a good style are also factors which have something to say when the problem is criticised, even if it is not solved exactly in the sense which presents itself to me as correct.

SOLUTION OF THE 60TH PROBLEM.

A. *Written solution by General v. Moltke.*

La Chapelle, 1st June, 1879, 6 p.m.
CORPS ORDER.

The 29th Division hands over 1 Squadron, 1 Battery, and the Engineer Company to the 58th Brigade, which is to stand south of Sermamagny ready to start to-morrow morning at 5 o'clock.

The Brigade advances to Valdoye, takes possession of that village, and at once intrenches itself behind the Savoureuse. The wooded heights d'Arsot and du Salbert will be occupied by Infantry. When this has been carried out, the Regiment 112 continues its march by the road round the northern foot of the Salbert to Chalonvillars, where it either awaits the arrival of the 57th Brigade or follows it.

The remaining troops of the Division advance to-morrow morning at 6 o'clock from south of Chaux by Sermamagny, Evette, Le Haut d'Evette to Chalonvillars, occupy the heights of Le Coudrai and La Côte on their front, and prepare Essert for defence.

The 28th Division, Corps Artillery as well as the 1st and 2nd Engineer Companies, assemble at La Chapelle at 6 a.m., and march by Errevet, Frahier, and Chagey as far as Buc—Echenans. The Advanced Guard, to be formed of all arms, occupies Urcerey and Argiésans. The Corps Artillery at the tail of the column halts at Chagey.

The Trains follow their troops in the afternoon.

The investment will be completed on the 3rd, by advancing the right wing as far as the lower Savoureuse.

Dispatched in writing : identically to the 28th and 29th Divisions. Verbally to the Commanders of the Artillery, the Trains and Commissariat.

B. *Verbatim shorthand report of General v. Moltke's verbal criticism.*

I thought I had given you a very easy problem, but it is surprising how few gentlemen have hit upon the right thing. I already took occasion at the last discussion to call your attention to the fact that one must not tie oneself down too stringently to general rules, but that departures from such are admissible. I think I have proved to you that in the former problem it was not absolutely necessary to form an Advanced Guard ; I should also like to convince you that it was here not necessary nor advisable to form a Reserve which in the event of an action was to move up as a reinforcement. A Reserve stands best behind the centre of the straight front, taking into consideration, of course, the roads and the ground ; a still more advantageous station is behind a line bent outwards, whence it can advance on any radius ; but the most inconvenient station is behind the convex line, *i.e.*, one curved inwardly. If you post the Reserve at Frahier, it has to march 4½ miles in order to support the left wing at Valdoye, and 9 miles to support the right wing, by Chagey to Echenans, further south. The Reserve will consequently arrive everywhere too late for action.

I think it therefore more practical to leave the units which are at our disposal, in this instance the Brigades, intact, so that they are as strong as possible, and each able to form its own reserve. To this end the Brigades must, of course, be made independent ; they must be provided with the special arms, which the Infantry Brigades, as matters stand, do not possess. I think you could apportion to each Brigade a Troop of Cavalry for orderly purposes, 2 complete Batteries, and ½ an Engineer Company ; in that case you retain the whole Corps Artillery and a part of the Engineers. The Engineer Battalion has, unfortunately, only 3 Companies of Sappers, which will be much wanted during the investment. A reserve of Sappers, of whom the General commanding could dispose, will, however, as a matter of course, be set free when the Brigades have taken up their defensive positions, and we see the ground and ascertain where extensive entrenchments are to be executed. We will then send them there, and send the Artillery to places where extensive positions for guns offer themselves.

I believe therefore that support by one's own and the neighbouring Brigades will be better and more rapidly insured than support from the General Reserve, which can find no favourable position here. Imagine that Valdoye is attacked before the Reserve arrives; it is then surely more advantageous if support comes from Cravanche against the enemy's flank. A sortie from the fortress is always very difficult; a small detachment acting on the flank will have a much greater effect than if 20 Battalions were stationed behind Valdoye; the enemy has always to bear in mind that he has to go back again into the fortress. Moreover, it must not be forgotten that the garrison, which is reinforced by only 1 mobile Brigade, has also to watch towards the east, and that the garrison at first is fully occupied with preparing and arming the fortress, that scarcely more than a Brigade will advance to attack, and that when we are established it will be very difficult for the enemy to push back even a single Brigade, if both neighbours are on the alert and ready to aid. But if it is absolutely wished to form a reserve, the distribution of the troops must head the Corps Order after first briefly explaining the general situation, so that each Brigadier knows what remains at his disposal.

Before we put ourselves in motion we must consider to what point we wish to march and where the positions are which we need for the investment. Valdoye then meets our eye first. It is a matter of regret to me that only very few gentlemen have occupied Valdoye ; it is certainly within the fire of the fortress ; but before Paris we went much nearer than within range. To stop this gap of Valdoye is for us of the very greatest importance. The eastern part of the investment has in its rear the railway, if that is not destroyed ; but we expect the whole of our materials by the northern road of Giromagny and Sermamagny. We must not allow that one to be interrupted, for by it will march during the following days large trains with provisions ; by it must be brought up—if the fortress is to be besieged—the whole Siege Train and the Ammunition Columns.

That road must therefore be secured under all circumstances ; but it is only secured if we occupy Valdoye and the wooded heights on both sides.   I would not rely, then, at all on the 1st Reserve Division, but say to myself: That village I occupy, and so also the east corner of the Forêt d'Arsot.   Therefore, capture we must Valdoye under all circumstances, and I would order a Brigade to do it, so that we may be sure of getting that village and the wooded heights.   It is sufficient if Valdoye is taken and rapidly put in a state of defence, quite as a small post, which gives us timely warning for taking up our position behind Valdoye, where we can deploy our whole Artillery.

It is now really indifferent whether the 29th Division stands on the left, the 28th on the right, or *vice versâ*.   It is natural that we have regard to the order of battle if the whole Army-Corps is together, that we therefore use the 28th Division on the south-west and the 29th on the north-west.   If I now assume that we are standing with the 29th Division on the north-west, the 58th Brigade would be designated to occupy Valdoye and the wooded slopes on both sides of the valley, and to keep them permanently occupied.,   With the remaining Brigades, it is true, we would have to make flank marches, in so far as the Brigades with numerous Artillery on mountain-roads present their left flank to the fortress, up to the moment when they have arrived at a point where they wheel to the left.   They can then rely upon themselves ; but so long as they are engaged in the forest-roads and marching in long columns it is necessary to cover their march.   The 28th Division is particularly affected by this as long as it is marching on Chagey, because from there it turns towards the fortress. The position next required for covering the movements appears necessary at Chalonvillars, and I would order the 57th Brigade to that place.   There is no doubt that the Brigades of the left wing can unhesitatingly take up their defensive positions already on the same day in the way they have to maintain them subsequently during the investment.

Some gentlemen who occupied Valdoye have been over-cautious ; they wished to delay the march until Valdoye was taken.   That has the disadvantage that the troops arrive too late, and that they have no time left for adopting the preliminary measures for defence.   It remains to be considered, at the same time, that a full hour will elapse before the whole Army-Corps gets into march ; therefore a Brigade of the 28th Division may still be available for supporting an action at Valdoye.

The 57th Brigade is to be put in motion at once by Evette on Chalonvillars, as most gentlemen have done, but—where is it to stand? I believe it is necessary to occupy Essert and the two wooded heights north and south of it. It certainly is still nearer to the fortress than Valdoye, but it would only be seen into perhaps from the Donjon; the height in front is 1,200 feet, the valley 1,100 feet. Yet should it be exposed to view we would have to confine ourselves to occupying the western part of Essert, but particularly the wooded heights on both sides—similarly as at Valdoye—for the possession of the village depends on these heights. If Essert is occupied we can take up a good defensive position in advance of Chalonvillars; that village must therefore certainly be occupied on the 2nd. You thus cover the whole march of the 28th Division, to which for convenience sake a special road must be assigned. It is to be found by Errevet and Frahier. Now, how far is the 28th Division to march? Some gentlemen said it should go as far as Héricourt or even Brévilliers. I do not consider that necessary. That is a march of 18 miles through the mountains, and there is no urgent reason for marching so far. If you assume the leading Brigade, the 56th, to advance by Chagey as far as Buc Mandrevillars and Echenans, the 55th on the other hand to halt in the neighbourhood of Chagey, Luze, and Couthenans, you have the whole Division assembled. Should the enemy make a sortie in that direction you are strong enough to repulse it. For the 3rd there remains then only an advance as far as the neighbourhood of Botans.

As regards the defensive position, it would still be very desirable for the 56th Brigade to advance at once as far as Buc, in order to occupy the heights in a northern direction as far as Chaufour; Valdoye, Essert, and Urcery would then indicate the line. It would be a question with the right Brigade, the 55th, whether one would push it out as far as Botans or retain it at Dorans. Afterwards it will advance to the Grand Bois, just as the investment on the other bank will proceed to Danjoutin. The last Brigade would arrive towards midday; whether it marches by Héricourt or takes the nearer road by Echenans depends on circumstances. The investment would thus be completed.

I should like to mention some further details. Several gentlemen wished to destroy the railway; but that is no part of the problem. We do not know where the Army is standing, nor whether we

have to reconnoitre as far as Vesoul or towards the south.   In order
to judge of that, all the circumstances connected with the Army, etc.,
would have to be precisely stated.   If in the problem nothing is said
about it you may assume that nothing is to be feared from that
quarter.   The destruction of railways is, moreover, a two-edged
sword,—it may be useless or very detrimental ; one must think twice
before doing it.

Some papers have not hit upon the solution as I have thought it
out for myself, but are very intelligent in judging the situation, which
still, however, leads sometimes to defective measures, e.g., it would be
quite impossible to remain at the halt between Evette and Chalonvillars before the wood of Salbert has been captured.   In some papers,
also, Artillery have got to the head of the columns, in consequence of
indistinct modes of expression.   But if a handful of Franctireurs is
ensconced in the woods it cannot get any further.

SOLUTION OF THE 61ST PROBLEM.

A. *Written solution by General v. Moltke.*

Advanced Guard : 3 Battalions, 3 Squadrons, 1 Battery, and
1 Ambulance Section, starts in good time, marches as Flank Guard
by Wever, Ober Tudorf, along the Haarweg, Cavalry ahead, and
opposes the enemy where he attempts to cross the Alme.

Main Body : 10 Battalions, 1 Squadron, 3 Batteries, and all the
Trains, in one column by the high-road, abreast of the Detachment,
the Squadron in advance, Trains in rear, Artillery behind the 3rd
Battalion.

Reinforcing the Detachment only so far as is necessary.

Defence, eventually, of the wooded district.   Breaking off the
action from the left wing, gaining the position Oster Schledde.

If the whole Division is obliged to deploy, the leading Regiment
of the Main Body makes a left turn ; while it is advancing the 10th
Brigade moves forward by the high-road into the second line.   The
Trains continue the march along the high-road in rear of the fight.

B. *Verbatim shorthand report of General v. Moltke's verbal criticism.*

The problem shows us the Division marching to the Rhine, and
in the first instance it is to march from Paderborn to Gesecke on the
2nd April ; perhaps its punctual arrival on the Rhine is of the

greatest importance. The march, therefore, is the main object upon which we have to direct our attention. We have no order to attack the enemy, who has shown himself south of Haaren ; we shall by no means go across the Alme and give battle. Our object is simply to march to Gesecke. Neither shall we occupy a position on the way for the enemy to attack us, if we can avoid it. If we cannot we will have to take care, as far as is possible at least, that we are not attacked in a position which is facing west, for then we could only continue our march after completely defeating the enemy. But we are not justified in supposing this, if the enemy, as is probable, is as strong as we are. We therefore shall, if obliged to take up a position, be it with a part, or be it with the whole Division, do so if possible with the front facing south-east, for then we fight only a Rear Guard action, and at the worst are pushed towards the object of our march. If we can at all avoid it, we shall do so ; but you see the problem already calls attention to a danger which could arise from the enemy, who has shown himself south of Haaren, throwing himself upon our line of march.

All the gentlemen have quite correctly recognised that it is necessary to secure the left flank, that opportunity for doing so is afforded by the apparently very considerable obstacle of the Alme, which runs pretty well parallel to our direction of march. Various means, however, have been proposed. If we first cast a glance on the map, we see that the distance from Paderborn to Gesecke is less than that from the south of Haaren to, let us say, Salzkotten, if the enemy, as is probable, takes the most direct road ; that is to say, if he advances by Wevelsburg.

We would accordingly have arrived with our leading troops in the neighbourhood of Gesecke when the enemy arrives at Upsprunge. But our column is more than 4½ miles long ; the enemy would therefore certainly encounter at least the rear of the column, if we do not take precautions. Defiling will certainly cost him time ; he must afterwards form up and advance with a deployed front ; but that is not sufficient ; he must encounter at those defiles an active resistance on our part.

Now, some papers have proposed to march with the whole Division along the Alme. That would, I think, not be advisable. If the column has a normal depth of more than 4½ miles it will extend to 9 miles going by the field-paths; it would need hours before the

L

rear could close on to the head. It will surely be much more easily able to support the Flank Guard if it remains with its Main Body on the high-road. Moreover, a large body, as, for example, a Division of all arms, does not leave the road unless absolutely obliged to do so.

Represent to yourselves the Flank Guard as fighting at Wevelsburg; you would then much more easily be able to support it from the high-road ; that distance is much shorter than the length of the column when marching by the field-paths. Now, if support of the Flank Guard is necessary, the 3 Battalions of the leading Regiment would simply make a left turn, and be at once ready for the Flank Guard to fall back upon at perhaps the southern edge of the zone of woods. The correct thing, we may say, is for the Main Body to remain on the high-road, and a strong Flank Guard to march along the Alme. Most of the gentlemen also have rightly understood that.

I will make a further interpolation here with a view to examining the situation : a Prussian Division is marching to the Prussian Rhine ; from that direction, therefore—though it is not expressly stated—surely no danger is to be apprehended. Notwithstanding, some gentlemen have thought the Division might be attacked from the south as well as at the same time from the west. But surely it cannot be my intention to lay a trap for you, gentlemen. Several gentlemen, nevertheless, sent a strong Advanced Guard of 3 to 4 Battalions, with Artillery and Cavalry, ahead by the high-road. It is, of course, in other circumstances a general rule that a body of troops does not march forward without an Advanced Guard ; but science does not give us a fundamental maxim which we must follow everywhere ; it does not give us a formula which helps us over all difficulties. In war the essential thing is to grasp every situation correctly, and to adopt the measures most appropriate to the situation.

Here, according to my opinion, we would not need an Advanced Guard at all ; our Advanced Guard is the Flank Guard which is marching in *that* direction where danger threatens. It is sufficient if a Troop of Dragoons is sent ahead in order to see what is going on. One must therefore under certain conditions know how to cast oneself loose from general rules. Advanced Guard and Main Body would here be in proper relation if any help was needed for the Flank Guard.

Now, most gentlemen have correctly recognised that they must form a strong Flank Guard for delaying the advance of the enemy; they have in some cases furnished it with 4 to 5 Battalions and 2 to 3 Batteries. I don't consider that necessary; 1 Regiment and 1 Battery would for the present be ample. It is also desirable to make the columns not too long; a small column marches more rapidly. Strangely enough, almost all gentlemen when doing so have understood the matter in such a way as to direct the leader of the Detachment to occupy a position. How can you know where the man has to take up a position? That depends upon the enemy. It is sufficient to say to the Commander of the Advanced Guard: You have to prevent the enemy crossing the Alme. He will then go of himself where the enemy is crossing. The man will be reasonable; he will not remain at Tudorf if the enemy is crossing at Ahden or somewhere else. But with a position, e.g., at the Stüssauer Teich or behind the Lohn with the wood close in front—how, in that case, will you regain contact with the Flank Guard if the column continues marching on? You would then have to halt with the Division at Salzkotten.

The Flank Guard, to which I would attach the whole of the Cavalry, will send it forward at a trot: it probably arrives on the Alme simultaneously with the enemy. If we assume the Advanced Guard of the Division to be at Wever on the evening of the 1st, it is standing nearer to Graffeln than the enemy, who is behind Haaren. Our Cavalry will probably arrive sooner at the defile than the enemy's Infantry, and will occupy it provisionally with dismounted Dragoons. The reports of the carbines will then apprise the Commander to what point he has to hasten his march.

It would not be right to indicate to the Detachment a point where it should halt while the enemy is crossing perhaps further up. If, nevertheless, the enemy could not be prevented from crossing the Alme, if he should have already a number of troops across (which is not probable), and if the Flank Guard were obliged to retire, the Division would be obliged to detach a force upon which it could fall back. I am even of opinion that at that time we would already be between Gesecke and Salzkotten, and would advance with a Regiment to the edge of the wood or with as much as we think necessary. We then have the retreat open to Gesecke; nothing further can happen to us than being slightly pressed, but we get to Gesecke. There we find a position which can be occupied, the Oster Schledde.

I have previously mentioned that one does not take up a posi-

L 2

tion *en route.* Now there exists a similarity in a group of papers which, all quite rightly, send a Flank Guard along the Alme, but which would, with the Main Body, take up an intermediate position behind Upsprunge—merely for the sake of the Trains ; these were to march on behind it. The Train is, however, not the main object, but the Division. You will require at least an hour for getting into the intermediate position, and then you expose the Division for several hours to the danger of being attacked by an equally strong enemy in a situation in which it has its rear against the bridge of the Lippe and the direction of march in prolongation of the flank. I don't consider that safe, and it is not necessary. Either the Flank Guard alone keeps back the enemy—the Division then continues marching unmolested—or you must support it ; then an action develops alongside the road.

To leave the Trains behind entirely would be a very bad measure We do not know at all yet whether the enemy will advance in the direction of Salzkotten. If he hears of the presence of a large column at Paderborn we hardly will see the Trains again.

I will just read to you my rough copy of the solution : The Division continues its march by Salzkotten on the 2nd April. The former Advanced Guard, brought up to 3 Battalions, 3 Squadrons, 1 Battery, and 1 Ambulance Section, advances as a left Flank Guard at 5 o'clock, by Wever and Ober Tudorf, along the Haarweg, the Cavalry at an accelerated rate in advance. The Detachment opposes the enemy where he will cross the Alme. (Thus full freedom is left to the Commander.)

The Main Body : 10 Battalions, 1 Squadron, 3 Batteries, 1 Engineer Company, with Divisional Pontoon Troop and 1 Ambulance Section, marches on a level with the Flank Guard, the Squadron in advance, Artillery behind the 3rd Battalion of the column, all Trains closing up immediately at the tail of the column. Reinforcing the Flank Detachment only so far as is necessary to be able to continue the march with the Main Body. Support for the Flank Guard at the southern edge of the woods. If it becomes necessary to deploy with the whole Division, the leading Regiment makes a left turn. While it is moving off the other Brigade moves by the road into its proper fighting position.

The Trains continue their march. Breaking off the action from the left wing. Gaining the section of ground behind the Oster Schledde.

SOLUTION OF THE 62ND PROBLEM.

A. *Written solution by General v. Moltke.*

The mere frontal advance against the apparently very tenable defiles of the Alme promises little success; at the best we force the enemy to an orderly retreat.

The Regiment No. 60, strengthened by 1 Battery and ½ a Squadron, marches through the Pröwenz wood, and posts itself under cover at Steinhaus.

The Division advances against Drei Eichen, the Advanced Guard deploys for action against that point.

From the attitude of the enemy's Advanced Guard it will soon be discerned whether he intends to continue his offensive or not.

If it offers vigorous resistance, the Main Body forms up in advance of the Oster Schledde, the Regiment No. 60 moves in the direction of Hännebols Linde on the flank of the columns advancing across the Alme, and the Main Body assumes the offensive at the proper moment.

If the Advanced Guard, after a slight skirmish, gives way before an attack, the Division continues its advance against the Alme, the Regiment No. 60 marches by Büren against the enemy's flank.

B. *Verbatim shorthand report of General v. Moltke's verbal criticism.*

The Division is charged with inflicting a defeat on the enemy if possible. I can imagine that this order was subjected to some criticism at headquarters in Gesecke. They would say: " We are to make the enemy suffer a defeat ; the enemy stands in a formidable position behind the river. How are we to set about this? It is our business to march to the Rhine. How far are we to run after him ? " The Commander-in-Chief is responsible for that order, but the Division for its execution. The Commander-in-Chief surely may also have had his reasons for issuing that order. It is perhaps very inconvenient for the Commander-in-Chief to see a hostile Division remaining so close to a road, which is perhaps to be a line of communication. The 60th Regiment is just available; it is handed over to us, and we are desired to provide against the above-mentioned inconvenience by a rapid blow. Willingly or unwillingly we will have to undertake the business after all.

Now we next would have to ask : What may the probable intentions of the enemy be ? And then we find that only two cases are possible. A third one is at once to be eliminated from consideration, namely, that the enemy withdraws without at all accepting battle. Then we can only report to headquarters that the enemy could not be made to suffer a defeat, because he is no longer there : that goes without saying. There remain, therefore, only two cases to be examined : either the hostile Division comes across the Alme in order to attack us, or it remains halting, and will defend itself behind the river. You will learn at once what the enemy's intentions are so soon as you attack the position at Drei Eichen. If there is in that position an Advanced Guard of a Division advancing to attack, it will accept the fight and carry it through to the end, sure of the arrival at any moment of the Division which is following in support. If, however, in the position at Drei Eichen the Rear Guard of a Division is standing which is halting or even retiring, it will not accept an action, certainly not in advance of the defile, but it will retire. Although you will learn the intentions of the enemy by this attack, yet that would be too late for adopting measures suitable to all cases. It will therefore be necessary to arrange matters from the beginning in such a way that they fit the one case as well as the other.

Some gentlemen made their resolutions dependent on a previous reconnaissance by the Cavalry. Thereby you surrender the initiative. The forenoon will pass, and by the Cavalry alone you will learn nothing ; for the enemy will not give up the position at Drei Eichen merely in the face of Cavalry. Still less can you expect the Cavalry to bring intelligence whether the enemy is marching back behind the Alme or not. It is better that you form your resolutions at once from the outset.

Some gentlemen have proposed a position in the neighbourhood of Gesecke ;—they wish to let the enemy come up, and then in turn to become offensive against him. Well, gentlemen, but if he does not come ? Shall we report : We have had the good intention of making the enemy suffer a defeat, but he did not come ? That will not do ; that would not be carrying out the order. It happens that in fact there is no position in the neighbourhood of Gesecke which could be at all recommended. The position at the Elsinger Warthe has the large wood of Pröwenz close in front. We do not learn that the enemy is moving against it ; but he will probably attack our right wing. Still less can we occupy a position further in advance with the wood closer in front. The position at Wester Warthe also in no way commends itself. The ground does not favour it ; the deep ravine rather divides the battlefield into two parts and interrupts the communications in rear of the position. Altogether I would not advise the occupation of a position at Gesecke which, the nearer it is taken up to our road, will bring that road the more in prolongation of our front, and, in case of an unsuccessful issue of the battle—which, surely, is always possible—would lead the Division northward across the road into very disagreeable terrain.

We are now justified in saying, that—although we have grown stronger by 3 Battalions, on account of the 60th Regiment being brought up, which may follow in Reserve or serve to prolong the front of attack—a purely frontal attack can hardly succeed against that position. We must certainly keep our forces collected on the northern bank of the Alme. If the enemy attacks us there, we must, in a measure, oppose to him an equal force. We then still retain an overplus of forces which we can use to advantage only against his flank, naturally only against his left flank. If you strengthen the 60th Regiment by a Battery of 4 guns, and allow it to advance as an independent Detachment against Steinhaus, it will render you there the very best services. It is quite understood that the Commander must be ordered—and he would also do so of his own accord—that, if the enemy advances across the Alme, he is to advance against his left flank ; that will stop the enemy's advance at once. The enemy will be obliged to detach a force towards his left, and thus make it easy for the Division to issue from the wood. If the enemy is standing behind the Alme, the Commander will have to seize Büren. Even if Büren is actually occupied by the enemy, he still has every prospect, owing to the formation of the defile here, of forcing his way in. He can then boldly advance against the enemy's left wing or against his communications. No misfortune can befall him ; he cannot be very much pressed in the wood, and has his line of retreat on Erwitte straight in rear. This advance will have the greatest influence on the maintenance of the position on the Alme. For the enemy necessarily must—as he cannot at all overlook what is coming against him in the wood—detach a force against it and weaken himself in front. That gives to the Main Body an opportunity of perhaps capturing the formidable bridges.

The question now is : How shall we dispose of the Main Body of the Division ? I am delighted to have seen very many of the gentlemen correctly grasping the idea, that we can fight only with a front facing east. They have caused an Advanced Guard to move against Drei Eichen, but they did so somewhat late, when getting into motion with the Main Body. They advance through the wood in several columns, with the left flank refused so that they can form front by a simple left wheel, if the enemy crosses the Alme. They thus place the enemy, after he has crossed, in a most critical situation : he is obliged to make a left turn, and has the defiles on his left flank. They have, indeed, every chance of gaining a decisive success. But if he remains behind the Alme, it is, according to my opinion, only possible to lay hold of him by Büren. Unfortunately, also, those gentlemen who have made such practical dispositions in the manner above described, have scarcely, or not at all, taken into consideration the second case, that of the enemy remaining behind the Alme. But surely that is absolutely necessary for carrying out the orders. Other gentlemen have arrived at different results. That cannot be wondered at ; different opinions may exist, if they are only brought out in a logical and clear manner.

SOLUTION OF THE 63RD PROBLEM.

A. *Written solution by General v. Moltke.*

The Detachment can oppose the enemy already on the heights behind Rezonville. But it has nothing to lean on there ; on the contrary it has the defile in rear, and will very soon be enveloped and driven back by the undoubtedly great superiority of the enemy.

A position at Gravelotte is somewhat better. The enemy is obliged to advance by the road under the fire of our Batteries or through the bottom of the valley under that of our skirmishers. The defence of the village and farms may detain him for hours. But when the Detachment finds itself in the end obliged to give up its position, its retreat will be a very difficult one. We must, moreover, consider that a renewed advance across the deeply-cut Mance valley will hardly be possible, even for the troops of the reinforced garrison.

A flanking position at Malmaison, front facing south, exposes the Detachment to the danger of being altogether unable to return again to Metz.

On the other hand, such a position at the Bois des Ognons facing north would most surely fulfil its purpose. Connection with Metz is ensured by two bridges at Ars sur Moselle.

The Battalions occupy the edge of the wood ; the Cavalry posts itself under cover east of the north corner of the wood. The Batteries stand at the corner of the wood protected from enfilade fire, and keep the road-bridge under a most effective fire, and the skirmishers pushed in advance render it difficult to cross the bottom of the valley. Even a support by the heavy ordnance from the high-lying forts, which are thus no longer masked by us, is not precluded, although the range is 6,000 metres.

The enemy is quite unable to gauge how strong we are in the wood. As long as we are stationed there on his flank he cannot establish himself on the plateau ; he must drive us away. Even after loss of the edge, such a fight in the wood, in which the enemy cannot make his superiority felt, may last the whole day long.

If the Detachment is not entirely driven across the Moselle on the 2nd, the Bois des Ognons is the most favourable line of approach for the reinforcements from the garrison of the fortress for recapturing the heights.

B. *Verbatim shorthand report of General v. Moltke's verbal criticism.*

The problem said that " Metz is threatened with siege," and that we are to prevent the enemy from taking possession of the plateau of Gravelotte. Well, with a weak force one cannot besiege Metz ; we may be, therefore, sure of the enemy arriving in considerable force. At least 80,000 to 100,000 men are required for the siege of Metz. Whether the heads only of such a force have provisionally arrived, whether they are advancing by one or by several roads, that is all unknown ; but we may assume with certainty that the enemy is greatly superior. Offensive proceedings can, therefore, hardly lead to any success, but may well lead to catastrophes. We must, therefore, make up for our weakness by using advantageous ground, and look for a defensive position.

There presents itself first the position on the height east of Rezonville. But that village lies in the valley, which there presents no frontal obstacle ; pivots for the wings do not exist at all, and there is no time for entrenchments. We will arrive at Rezonville perhaps simultaneously with the enemy. Moreover, the position can be turned on all sides : the enemy can advance by the Römer Strasse and envelop our right wing. The intention of those gentlemen who

have taken up that position is intrinsically quite correct : they wish
to force the enemy to an early deployment, and thus to gain time
which is certainly of importance. But it makes a great difference
whether a strong or quite a weak body is acting in that way. In the
former case, if we oblige, for instance, an Army-Corps, marching by
one road, to deploy, it takes 3 to 4 hours ; but the enemy will
deploy here only with his Advanced Guard. The deployment of 5
or 6 Battalions does not take long, and if we then have to move off
we have gained little time. But, if we accept battle, we run the risk
of being followed at once by the enemy. He need not for this
purpose break off the engagement ; he can follow us deployed for
action, and arrive simultaneously with us on the plateau of Gravelotte. But if we wish to retire slowly, and repeatedly to face
about, it is illusory, and would certainly not be done in actual
warfare.

A second position is that behind the upper valley of the Gorze
brook. Those gentlemen who occupied that position have placed
their Artillery on the heights 956 and 964. That is quite right,
for the Artillery must advance close to the edge in order to keep
the convex slope of the ravine under fire. But that position is commanded by the opposite bank, and in front of the right wing there
lies the wood, which it is impossible for us to occupy with our small
force. If the enemy penetrates as far as this, he drives away our
Artillery with Infantry fire. The right wing is altogether most in
danger ; a long resistance, I believe, will not be possible here either.

The position at Gravelotte—Mogador after all keeps the forces
concentrated, and we have ample time to fortify it. Both roads join
there, an envelopment of the position is therefore more difficult for
the enemy, but we have a formidable defile immediately in rear. If
the enemy envelops our right wing (it is supposed that we have
occupied Malmaison for observation and that those troops afterwards withdraw again to Gravelotte) and advances as far as the
hollow road, retreat becomes impossible. But, in case we go back
betimes to the plateau of St. Hubert, every prospect of an offensive
subsequently vanishes, if on the next day the complete war garrison
arrives.

All the gentlemen have rightly recognised and expressed the
difficulties of all these positions ; but, notwithstanding that, they
thought they must occupy at least the best of them. I can imagine

that they said to themselves, This is a curious problem ; it cannot be solved at all. I also believe that no position facing the enemy answers the purpose. But we can perhaps elude the enemy.

Let us figure to ourselves for one moment the idea of a flanking position. A flanking position is a position which is taken up near and parallel to the enemy's line of operation—a position which the enemy cannot pass without laying open his lines of communication—a position which he cannot attack without changing his front, thus getting his communications on his flank—a position where a victorious action and a pursuit divert him from his original object. At the same time we must consider of course that we also abandon our line of retreat. A flanking position can therefore as a rule only be taken up in our own country, where a friendly hinterland exists upon which we can live. That will be much more difficult in an enemy's country. We, moreover, offer one wing to the enemy ; it is therefore a condition that this wing finds a strong support in the ground—otherwise the enemy advances obliquely, and thence rolls up our position.

Several flanking positions have been taken up. Firstly, one facing south in the wood alongside the Römer Strasse. But the edge of that wood is 3,000 paces long ; an adequate occupation is therefore not possible. The right wing finds no other support but the edge of the wood, and the enemy would very soon take possession of the corner of the wood. If he should advance thoughtlessly against Rezonville, an opportunity would perhaps be found of creating much confusion among his Advanced Guard by a sudden rush forward. A particular success, however, would not be gained thereby. Another flanking position was taken up at Malmaison. The same holds good for that one as for the former. Those gentlemen who have selected one of these positions should have made one thing clear to themselves : namely, that, if they accept battle, they could not count upon getting back into Gravelotte by a left turn. They would have got back into Metz perhaps by a roundabout way through Chautrenne and then by Woippy ; but there is always a danger attending it.

Somewhat better is a flanking position in the neighbourhood of Flavigny, facing north, and with its line of retreat, although by decidedly circuitous roads, just behind it. The enemy will then certainly be obliged to deviate from his original direction ; but the

plateau of Gravelotte remains perfectly open. The position is, more-over, too far in advance, and the march to it exceedingly difficult. If we advance by the high-road, an encounter with the enemy may take place already at Rezonville; but hardly any roads at all lead through the wood.

Thus, after all, no other choice is left but Occupation of the northern edge of the Bois des Ognons. Gentlemen, imagine the edge of that wood occupied by two Battalions deployed in company columns with firing-line in front, in the square re-entering portion a Battery protected against enfilade fire from the other bank. A road leads from there straight to the rear. If that wood-path is im-passable for Artillery both Batteries would find a position near the north-east corner of the wood. That is also just the place for the Cavalry, which naturally at first remains at Rezonville for observa-tion; it stands there perfectly screened.

That position fulfils the primary conditions required of a flanking position. Besides the paths through the wood, there is the high-road to Ars in its rear, where two bridges are found. The river itself secures the connection with Metz. The left wing leans for support on the ravine of the Gorze brook. However, you will say to me now : " But Gravelotte remains thus quite open, and while the enemy attacks us he steps on to the plateau ! " That is quite right ; but he does not possess it. As long as he must expect to be attacked at any moment from the wood on his flank, he cannot establish on the plateau either Artillery or Engineer Park. He cannot judge, more-over, what there is in the wood, and he is continually threatened until he has complete possession of the wood. We have nothing to fear from an occupation of the heights of St. Hubert; the enemy comes there under fire from the forts of Metz. The enemy can do nothing else but attack us and drive us away. He will advance on both sides of the road through the valley ; on the plateau he will execute a right wheel under the fire of our Artillery, and then attack the edge of the wood, which is defended by our Infantry, and which we can have strengthened at our leisure.

I anticipate that the enemy will first post himself under cover of the undulations, move up his Artillery, and wait until sufficient forces have come up, in order to attack our left wing simultaneously with the front. If we lose the edge of the wood we naturally must go back, and will then slowly retire as far as the bend of the high-road. A perfectly parallel action then ensues in this bush, which is difficult to pass on account of the dense undergrowth. The paths leading through it are continuous defiles ; the enemy therefore cannot make use at all of his superiority; at the most he can only bring up from behind more and more reinforcements in order to fill the gaps in front. But also we have a Battalion still in Reserve. Cavalry and Artillery he cannot use at all any longer, after his skirmishers have gained the edge of the wood ; an envelopment is not possible, as we have deep ravines to the left and right.

Thus the affair turns out to be on equal terms, and it will be an arduous advance step by step. In this way the fight can be dragged along till dark, and if we even maintain ourselves only at the southern edge there is left the possibility of resuming from there the offensive to-morrow, when reinforcements arrive. That will at least be more easily done from there than by the defile of Gravelotte. In that manner the difficult task is best accomplished. From those gentlemen, who have not hit upon it, several good papers have been handed in, which show a clear intelligence and a trained military eye for the ground.

SOLUTION OF THE 64TH PROBLEM.

A. *Written solution by General v. Moltke.*

The occupation of the gently sloping range of heights east of Blumberg, extending about 5,000 paces from the Döring lake, about as far as the Kibitz lake, corresponds with the strength of the hostile Army Corps, at the same time permitting the retention of sufficient Reserves in a covered position. The frontal attack on that position will entail exceedingly great losses owing to the effect of the enemy's fire, who in all probability is covered by shelter-trenches and gun-emplacements.

On the other hand, the configuration of the ground permits us to maintain the line Seefeld—Krummensee with comparatively small forces against probable offensive enterprises of the enemy, and to employ a considerable part of the Army Corps for an attack on one or the other of his wings. The patches of wood in front of both facilitate an approach. Now, the envelopment of the enemy's right wing would at best drive him only on his line of retreat, while an advance against his left soon threatens his line of communications, which will not remain without reacting on the defence of the main position.

Therefore, the 4th Division will be charged with the defence of our front.

The 7th Infantry Brigade moves into a covered position behind the Fenn Berg. Its skirmishers are pushed out as far as the high-road, where they entrench themselves, in so far as that road and the strip of wood do not already afford sufficient cover. Only a post of observation is sent to Krummensee, but a Battalion is posted at Seefeld. It furnishes the escort for three Batteries of the Divisional Artillery, which from the Spitz Berg will engage the enemy's Artillery.

The 8th Brigade, the Corps Artillery, and the 3rd Cavalry Brigade, form a Reserve at the Ziegelei, at the road from Seefeld to Werneuchen, in order to reinforce, according to the course of the action, the front or to support the attack of the right wing.

The 3rd Division is designated to carry out that attack. Three Batteries of its Artillery unlimber on the height close to and north of Löhme.

The Infantry of the Division advances in echelon in such a manner that the 5th Brigade with a Battery forms the furthermost echelon on the right wing. It occupies the wood south of Reh Bruch, and advances from there to attack the woods at Helenenau with skirmishers and supports, the Battalions eventually following close behind.

The 6th Brigade conforms to that movement on the left, maintaining connection with the 4th Division. As soon as the Batteries at Löhme are thereby masked they move up nearer to the wood.

The General commanding will attend to reinforcing with the Corps Artillery ; he will also notice the proper moment for probable action of the Cavalry Brigade, and finally determine when the 7th Brigade is to proceed with the frontal attack according to the progress of the right wing at the Christinen Heide.

B. *Verbatim shorthand report of General v. Moltke's verbal criticism.*

Gentlemen, The situation as stated in the problem is evidently exceedingly unfavourable for the hostile Army Corps. We may well assume that it is surprised at the approach of the 2nd Army Corps, that it received intelligence of its advance towards Werneuchen only after it had already, as stated in the problem, moved through Bernau in the forenoon, and that the superior strength of the 2nd Army Corps is unknown to it. Now, the hostile Corps, as it could not do otherwise, has at once turned from Bernau to the left and occupied a position at Blumberg facing east, and that is, according to my opinion at least, not at all an unfavourable position. For, surely, it cannot be looked upon as a considerable disadvantage if the ground rises a few metres in a distance of 1,000 paces. The position has an excellent field of fire on all sides. The right wing, certainly, does not find any support from the ground, but it does not matter; that defect can be remedied by a Battery on the height 235. The bulk of the Corps stands screened behind the heights, and can move from that place under cover in all directions. Some embarrassment is felt on the left wing, in so far as a complete occupation of the patches of wood in advance cannot be undertaken without weakening too much the defence of the front. It is of course a very great disadvantage that the lines of communication are situated completely on the flank.

I daresay it is evident that the hostile Corps cannot march to-morrow on Berlin. Even if the 2nd Corps does nothing whatever, and remains completely passive, it would still be a desperate situation to advance against a town of a million inhabitants while a superior body of troops is standing immediately in rear. We therefore have no reason whatever for pushing ourselves between Berlin and the enemy.

If we place ourselves now in the enemy's position, he can in the first instance collect all his forces and offensively advance on Werneuchen. If he succeeds in driving us from our present position, the conditions for his lines of communication improve at the same rate as he progresses. The further he penetrates beyond Werneuchen the more he gets his communications on Bernau into his rear; if he finally succeeds in completely defeating us, the road to Berlin is also open to him.

How he would fare in such an enterprise, that is a different question. It would certainly not be the first time that a weak body defeated a stronger one, especially if the latter has previously weakened it by detaching largely. That case is improbable, but still possible, and we cannot disregard it entirely. We also have to take care of our lines of communication: we are standing with our back towards the Oder, over which there is no bridge from Cüstrin to Schwedt, and we also must execute a kind of lateral movement if we are beaten. In any case we must protect our Trains.

Another enterprise, or rather a different proceeding, of the hostile Corps would be to do nothing at all, remaining in its position and awaiting a frontal attack. Then the consideration becomes paramount that in case of misfortune affairs with the enemy would take a very unfavourable turn. He might be pushed away in a direction which must have for him the gravest consequences. That case is therefore still more improbable.

The enemy will try to extricate himself from that embarrassing situation as soon as possible. That is of course not possible without fighting; the Corps are too near for that. How would the enemy now be able to execute that retreat? He probably will leave his Batteries for the present in position and accept the Artillery duel, he will demonstrate with Infantry on the heights, and withdraw it only after the Main Body has departed. He has 3 roads to retreat by : Blumberg—Börnicke, Blumberg—Bernau, and the road leading to Birkholz, and then into the high-road. His columns are thus considerably shortened. Everything will depend upon the patches of wood being maintained between Löhme and Börnicke. If he has to deploy for action, which can be done by the 3 columns simply making a right turn, he is formed in 3 lines which can support each other. But he will do that very reluctantly, and continue marching as long as possible. Therefore everything with him depends on gaining time.

From that immediately follows what we have to do. If we have bivouacked opposite the enemy we naturally have placed outposts somewhere in a line, Löhme—Seefeld—Krummensee. We will have to arrange our measures for the above-mentioned three cases, and the strength which we give to the different bodies will be regulated by the probability of these three cases respectively.

First of all the securing of our front. It is only natural if we apportion the Brigade of the left wing to that duty. Some have apportioned the 6th Brigade to it ; no exception can be taken to that, if it was stationed on the left wing,—but then it ought to have been specially stated that such was the assumption. We employ the 8th Brigade to do so, strengthened by the Divisional Cavalry Regiment The Brigade finds a favourable defensive position on the so-called Hohen Graben. The Cavalry observes towards the enemy beyond Krummensee. The Artillery will be placed with 2 Batteries both behind the Fenn Berg and behind the Spitz Berg, whence they flank the whole front in case of attack. Some gentlemen have pushed the Artillery more forward, but it then stands under a convergent fire of the hostile Batteries. The Brigade has two other duties besides: 'to occupy the enemy and to detain him in his position. That is of course not to be done by advancing in mass, but in the first instance by skirmishers, who will surely find some cover on the ground. It would finally have to carry out the frontal attack, but in order to avoid unnecessary losses, not before the action on the opposite wing makes itself felt. These are the duties of that Brigade. If it discovers that the enemy intends to withdraw it will of course advance at once.

It is the simplest to designate the 7th Brigade as a Reserve. It is best placed behind Löhme, where it can reinforce the 8th Brigade and also support the right wing. From Löhme it can advance also on the flank of an eventual attack by the enemy.

We have the whole 3rd Division now available for advancing against the enemy. Several gentlemen have quite correctly designated the 3rd Division for that object, but they advance with it by Weesow, Wilmersdorf and Börnicke. That is a march of 4½ miles; they lose much time thereby which benefits the enemy. It has, moreover, the disadvantage of dividing the Army Corps into two parts without connection; for the Reserve Brigade is insufficient for upholding that connection. Some gentlemen caused additional bridges to be constructed across the Igel Pfuhl; but that is not at all necessary; between Igel Pfuhl and Löhme there is room enough for 2 Brigades If we deploy the 6th Brigade with its left wing at Löhme we have a position for 3 Brigades in close contact and with a Brigade in Reserve. The 5th Brigade deploys then for attack further north, in order to envelop the enemy.

It is here not a question of making a turning movement, but of executing an envelopment by the shortest road past the right of Löhme. The 5th Brigade then advances against the Fenn Fichten, the 6th against the Reh Bruch. If the patches of wood are not occupied, so much the better—they are serving then as pivots for a further advance; if they are occupied, we have Artillery enough for preparing the attack. It depends on how rapidly we take possession of all those patches of wood and what success we gain. The right column of the enemy will probably no longer get to Bernau; it will have to give way beyond Zepernick or Buch, and try to rejoin its Corps behind the Panke.

M

There are several papers which have not adopted exactly the same measures which I propose, but which are clearly and logically written, and from which a correct military judgment may be inferred. That is the main point ; for in war as well as in art there is no fixed rule ; talent cannot in either be replaced by a regulation.

SOLUTION OF THE 65TH PROBLEM.

A. *Written solution by General v. Moltke.*

(*Verbal criticism vide 66th Problem.*)

(To 1.) The Detachment bivouacs near the wood between Langguther and Lobe lakes. Outposts on the Passarge, piquet in Langguther Mühle.

(To 2.) Timely start : 6 o'clock.

The Dragoons and the Battery No. 1 at an accelerated pace ahead. Two of their Squadrons, until the arrival of Infantry, occupy the patches of wood on the line of lakes between Eissing and Mahrung lakes, 4 guns behind Ramten—Locken Teich (Mühlen T.).

Two Squadrons continue the march, and in the same way occupy the section between Mahrung and Narien lakes, 2 guns east of Horn.

The Infantry Brigade marches by the road to Mohrungen in the order of battle in one body, the Battery between both Regiments (at the present without Advanced or Rear Guards). Rifles in rear.

The outposts follow so soon as the column has passed Worleimen.

This side of Locken the leading Battalions I. and II. of the Regiment No. 21 turn to the right, relieve the 2 Dragoon Squadrons, and eventually take up a position behind Locken—Mühlen Teich. If necessary : reinforcing by the Rifle Battalion and guns from the Main Body. These Detachments follow the Main Body as soon as it has reached Eckersdorf, and from that moment form the Rear Guard.

From Eckersdorf the Fusilier Battalion of Regiment No. 21 goes eastward round Horn, in order to occupy the section hitherto held by the Dragoons.

The Main Body marches westward round Horn, and takes up a position north of it until the Corps has passed Himmelforth, draws in all the Detachments, and eventually falls back fighting on Himmelforth —Pfeilings.

SOLUTION OF THE 66TH PROBLEM.

A. *Written solution by General v. Moltke.*

The field of attack of the Eastern Corps is limited by the Narien lake and the Passarge, and lengthwise divided into two halves by the lake-valley of Banners—Lettau—Waltersdorf. The assailant will have to decide whether to advance concentrated along one of those sections or separated along both.

If he has knowledge of a large Detachment of his enemy standing at Herzogswalde he will scarcely advance with all his forces against the front of Liebstadt—Pittehnen, because that Detachment when advancing between Milden and Wuchsnig lakes would take his attack in flank and rear. He would be obliged to move a considerable part of his forces through Lettau against that Flank Guard in order to occupy and to detain it; he would arrive before the main position of the 2nd Corps weakened, and the attack on it would still depend on success at Herzogswalde.

If the Eastern Corps would rather determine to advance with all its assembled forces against the Flank Detachment, the latter could certainly be pushed back notwithstanding the favourable ground. It will then not withdraw between both lakes—thus masking the front of its own Corps—but, still fighting, join its right wing by Workallen. Any pursuit, however, would be brought to a standstill by an offensive advance of the Main Body by way of Achthuben. An advance of the Main Body straight forward on Banners should oblige the Eastern Corps to retrace its steps at once on account of the position of its lines of communication.

Hardly any other choice is therefore left to the Eastern Corps but to divide its forces.

The Main Body directed against Herzogswalde does not strike the vital part of the enemy, and endangers the lines of communication. The Flank Guard has therefore to expect only a secondary attack, which it has to sustain on favourable ground, always ready to fall with its Reserves upon the flank of the main attack. It does not so very much matter whether that is done in more or less strength. Only after the Flank Detachment is pushed back beyond Alt Bolitten does the mutual flank defence between Detachment and Main Body cease. The former will therefore not immediately join the Main Body on the 3rd of April, but remain in its exceedingly favourable position and establish and maintain itself there to the best of its power.

M 2

B. *Verbatim shorthand report of Lieutenant-General Count v. Waldersee's verbal criticism (representing General v. Moltke).*

Gentlemen, An Army-Corps is endeavouring to effect a junction with another which is also advancing and about three or four days' marches distant. It ascertains that a hostile Army-Corps is uncomfortably near its right flank. It consequently turns somewhat to the left in order to avoid, as much as possible, contact with the enemy, and charges a Detachment, a combined Brigade, with protecting its march. That is the situation upon which both problems are based.

The two tasks demanded from the Brigade are of essentially different nature on the 2nd and 3rd April. While on the 2nd it is a question of covering the Army-Corps during its march, and of avoiding at the same time as much as possible any fighting, in order that the Army-Corps may not have to face about and become engaged in an action, it is on the 3rd a matter of protecting, in the first instance, the Army-Corps which is forming up, of covering its deployment therefore, and so far from avoiding an action, even of bringing one about, at least on no account of evading it, and thereby giving the Army-Corps time to complete its deployment, and thus preventing its being drawn into a serious action even on that day, the reason for this being that the 1st Army-Corps can only in the evening arrive abreast of our Corps.

If we look at the ground we find the Army-Corps separated from the enemy by the Passarge. The latter is at that part of its course a rather unimportant little stream and not a considerable obstacle. That is also apparent from the fords which can be recognised at several places by the roads leading up to them and continuing on the other bank. It is altogether difficult for a Detachment of so little strength to undertake the protection of such a long river line; the course of the Passarge is also unfavourable in so far as it bends to the right when on a level with the Mahrung lake, and therefore approaches the enemy. He would be able to cross the river before we are in a position to oppose it. But the Eissing, Mahrung, and Narien line of lakes, running parallel to the Passarge and to the direction of the march of the Army-Corps, forms a prominent feature. These lakes cover the Corps on the flank; between them there are only two defiles. It will therefore come to this, that the Detachment bars these defiles against the enemy. The great majority of the gentlemen have certainly hit upon the right thing by laying stress upon the defile of Locken. They have endeavoured to take post there, in order to await the enemy in the first instance, and then to resume the march after a certain time. Just as important, however, is the defile between Mahrung and Narien lakes. This was not sufficiently recognised by many gentlemen. The enemy can push forward there just as well as further south. We do not know where the enemy was met. The problem tells us : at Allenstein. That does not mean that the intelligence is true ; the enemy can have also advanced further to Deppen; he can construct bridges and attempt an advance there or further up.

I now turn to the measures for the evening of the 1st April. I have chosen this line of argument because I wish gentlemen to see that, although we had different tasks for the 1st and 2nd of April, both had still to be considered together. They are most intimately connected. Get used to keeping in view the duties also for the following day when adopting the measures for the evening. One must try to arrange the quarters for the Detachment for the night in such a way that time and distance are gained thereby for the march on the following day.

If gentlemen had taken that into account they would probably have selected the bivouac of the Detachment further to the rear than they have done. The right place for it is between Langguther and Lobe lakes. It can here be altogether only a question of bivouacking, for we are in the neighbourhood of the enemy. If we wished to move into cantonments much time would be lost in the evening on the one hand, and on the other much time would also be required for collecting the Detachment on the following morning, and the troops would thus have less rest in cantonments than in a bivouac. Truly, bivouacking in East Prussia on the 1st of April is not a pleasure. The map is partly very indistinct, and may have rendered the problem more difficult for the gentlemen ; particularly the course of the Passarge which runs through the Langguther lake is not easily recognised.

We have arrived at Langguth with the intention of continuing the march. We must therefore cross the Passarge at the Langguther Mühle and place it between ourselves and the enemy, owing to which our measures of security are very much simplified. Some gentlemen have selected a bivouac south of Langguth, and many gentlemen have chosen cantonments, causing thus an undue extension. The most suitable place in all the circumstances is between the two lakes mentioned.   If there is a place near Lobkeim, billets may be drawn in that village.   As regards measures of security, an occupation of Langguther Mühle would really suffice.   But it would commend itself to push the outposts farther, in order to keep open the defile at all events.   A natural outpost position is the course of the Alte Passarge.   If we push out there about 2 Companies with a few orderlies and occupy with 1 Company Langguther Mühle, we have done all that is wanted.   Many gentlemen have gone too far as regards the number of troops for the outposts, up to a third of the total strength.   These are manœuvre ideas.   We there wish to practise, if possible, all our troops in outpost duty ; that is the reason for the regulation that at the manœuvres of Detachments a third of the strength is to be used for that duty.   In real warfare we must try to do it with as few troops as possible, for they have no rest at night. The fewer, the better.   Here, 3 Companies with a few Troopers will go a long way.   Moreover, very much Cavalry was attached to the outposts.   There is no object in that.   Cavalry also needs rest. Reconnaissances by Cavalry were also ordered for the evening even. Imagine patrols advancing at night on that ground ; they are fired upon somewhere in the wood, they have to return, and know just as much as before.   Leave them in peace.   For reconnaissance we need daylight.

Then, some gentlemen have ordered additional measures for the evening.   Frequently great value has been attached to the defile of Pulfnick, and they were anxious to reach and to occupy it that very evening.   The wording of the problem : "The Detachment after a long march on country roads," etc., means that the troops are tired and must have rest ; no further movements can therefore take place. Movements even to Locken only are inadmissible.   Give rest to the troops to-day and start early to-morrow morning.   It is not likely that the enemy will forestall you.   His patrols withdrew on Alt Schöneberg ; he does not like to march at night either.

An order was also given to destroy bridges on the same evening, especially that at Pulfnick.   At the same time it was overlooked that two fords lead at that bridge across the Passarge ; the demolition is therefore to no purpose.   The Engineer Company was also sent abroad alone during the night with the order to destroy bridges. That is inadmissible.   The Cavalry also was frequently charged with demolishing bridges.   The Cavalry generally cannot do that ;

for one does not known whether the bridges are of stone or of wood. Those are measures which are easily adopted on paper, but rarely executed in reality.

If we summarise the measures for the evening then I propose : Crossing of the Detachment at the Langguther Mühle, going into bivouac at a suitable place between Lobe and Langguther lakes, outposts at the most 3 Companies, for the remainder rest.

The next morning an early start must be made in any case. It is the 1st of April, somewhat after the equinox ; the sun rises at 5.35 ; towards 5 o'clock it begins to grow light. A march before that time is therefore a perfect night march. I propose 6 o'clock; we then have had daylight for an hour, the troops have time to get ready and to cook during daylight, only the mounted troops will have to be astir somewhat sooner.

It is a question of reaching the defile between Eissing and Mahrung lakes in time to bar it against the enemy. That defile is connected with the Passarge bridge at Pulfnick. Several gentlemen have transferred their defence to there. The ground is, however, not quite suitable for it, as the Passarge on the right bank is bordered by woods. We are not able to ascertain the enemy's advance : he reaches the river unmolested. We stand there also somewhat cramped, and have our line of retreat through an awkward defile. Give up the idea, therefore ; you stand better and more concentrated on the plateau near Locken with the lowlands of the lakes in front of you. If you make up your mind to receive the enemy there you would, I feel sure, do right.

But we must appear there early. Some gentlemen have therefore sent Cavalry ahead, and ordered it to occupy a position provisionally. But nobody made up his mind to attach Artillery to that Cavalry. An idea prevails that Cavalry can only be accompanied by Horse Artillery. That is not the case; Field Artillery is also able for this duty. But attaching Artillery has here a great significance, for you are to delay the enemy. If a few Squadrons are standing there, fighting on foot perhaps, the enemy will go boldly forward, as carbine fire is all he gets ; he will hardly suffer any long delay. But if you imagine Artillery distributed, you can receive the enemy with shells soon after he has crossed the bridge at Pulfnick. This causes a halt ; the enemy will not march boldly forward without taking any further notice, but he will reconnoitre first. Time is thereby gained, and that is just what we want. And so much time must be gained that the Detachment is able to come up. Let the Dragoon Regiment therefore advance early, at an accelerated pace, and attach a Battery to it. The Regiment takes post behind the line of lakes with the Artillery ready for action, and awaits the enemy.

The Detachment itself marches without any further subdividing, because the Dragoon Regiment is its Advanced Guard. Also a Rear Guard is hardly necessary, the outpost troops forming it quite naturally when joining in the march at the proper distance. Let the Detachment, therefore, march closed up by the high-road in one column of route, the 2* Batteries perhaps behind the leading Battalion, all closed up. Several gentlemen have left some troops behind at Langguth to stay there for some time. That is to no purpose; neither is the consideration whether the enemy could push on by Langguth. If he does so we can calmly let him push; he meets then only the tail of the Army-Corps, which has sent its baggage in advance. If the enemy comes in contact with our Rear Guard he only does what we wish him to do: he drives us towards our object. We have no inducement to render that movement difficult for him. He will probably not be able to advance even to Locken if he ascertains that we are standing there; he has to detach a force, or his advance will be delayed.

Just as it is necessary to have troops at the defile of Locken, so also is it necessary to appear with troops in time between the other two lakes, viz.: east of Horn. As soon as the Detachment reaches Locken with the leading troops, it will be desirable to throw a part of the Cavalry and Artillery farther forward, in order to face the enemy between the two lakes and to await him there. If you send perhaps 2 Squadrons with 2 guns they could act in the same manner as was the case at Locken. That does not give absolute protection, but the mere appearance of those troops will have the desired effect.

The question now is, How long we shall remain at those defiles. Many gentlemen have made a calculation which is mostly correct; but we must keep in constant communication with the Army-Corps, as we must know where it is at any moment, in order not to err. We have to arrange accordingly the moving forward of the Detachment at Locken for the occupation of the defile at Horn.

---

* The wagons of the 2nd Battery, which is attached to the Cavalry, must be meant here, as there are only 2 Batteries.—TRANSLATOR.

In addition to these measures it will still be necessary to continue reconnoitring towards the enemy. A few patrols, however, are quite sufficient for that purpose. Some gentlemen have sent forward the whole Dragoon Regiment, others some Squadrons. I propose to send only patrols, who will have to move in the direction of Seubersdorf. We must of course from the outset reconnoitre also towards Alt Schöneberg. These patrols have to remain constantly on the ground in advance, and to observe the march of the enemy. If it is ascertained that the enemy is crossing at or above Kallisten on that day, the Detachment at Locken will still have time to bar his advance at Horn. If he crosses at Pulfnick and attacks Locken, the duration of the resistance will have to be gauged by the numbers with which he does so. The ground is well adapted for a Rear Guard action. We evacuate the first position, withdraw behind the Locken brook, and afterwards to Eckersdorf. We find everywhere supporting points for the flanks, we cannot be enveloped, and we make in any case a slow retreat.

Some gentlemen have taken notice of the defile at Gross Hermenau. That is situated in advance of the Army-Corps which is on the march, and has nothing to do with the problem. When other gentlemen resolved to march from Langguth forward against the enemy, they made a mistake, since the problem says: "to avoid an action as much as possible."

The day has now passed without the Detachment being attacked either at Locken or at Horn. The Army-Corps has executed the march to Mohrungen. It will on the 3rd of April march on Liebstadt, and again be accompanied by the Detachment on its right flank. The patrols establish in the morning that the enemy in considerable strength has moved to Deppen, and had bivouacked at Schlitt. After an early start of the Detachment, and while it is marching to Herzogswalde, the further news arrives that the enemy intends to cross at Deppen. He is constructing some other bridges in addition to those already existing there—a sign that he will effect a crossing with large bodies of troops.

The Detachment, according to the problem, has arrived at Herzogswalde and occupied the Ponarien forest with the Rifle Battalion. It is not stated in the problem where the Cavalry is. If, however, gentlemen will imagine their situation they will find that its place is on the right flank. I would have therefore sent forward the

whole Cavalry Regiment to the heights at Seubersdorf, whence it can observe the enemy; it can eventually move still farther to Waltersdorf. It is a question of hiding as much as possible our own movements from the enemy's view. The Army-Corps is to deploy at Liebstadt. If hostile patrols get as far as Banners they can overlook the deployment. That must be prevented. The Dragoon Regiment must therefore be instructed to advance to Seubersdorf to watch the enemy from a suitable spot, to reconnoitre his march, but at the same time to prevent an advance of the hostile Cavalry on Banners, so as to veil our own movements.

The enemy's advance must be considered in regard to a strip of ground more than $4\frac{1}{2}$ miles broad between Passarge and the line of the larger lakes. That strip is again divided into two sections by the smaller line of lakes stretching from Waltersdorf to the Wuchsnig lake. The ground on each of these sections forms a kind of ridge, which slopes down towards the lines of lakes and the Passarge. That is nearly how the ground appears to me ; at any rate the high-road Waltersdorf—Liebstadt runs along the top of the eastern ridge. By the problem we know that the Detachment is left without instructions. It only knows that the Army-Corps, which reaches Liebstadt with the leading troops at 10 o'clock, will deploy there and await the 1st Army-Corps, which is advancing from Wormditt on the other bank of the Passarge, but which can only arrive at Schwenkitten in the evening. The distance from Kallisten to Liebstadt is about 7 miles. The reports say that the enemy has crossed the Passarge at 10 o'clock and deployed on both sides of the Waltersdorf highroad. If the enemy begins his advance unmolested he will undoubtedly reach the Corps about midday. He will either force it to fight or oblige it to evade him. It will rest with the Detachment to prevent this advance of the enemy, which is so dangerous.

It must therefore accept the fight independently. We must ask now, What are the chances of such a fight ? The ground, as we have seen, is divided into two parts by the line of little lakes. The enemy can advance on the right or on the left section, or he can divide and advance on both. His tendency must be, if he calculates rightly, to reach the Army-Corps as early as possible, and to hurl it in a direction that will render its junction with the 1st Army-Corps impossible. That will induce him to advance on the right section. He then encounters the left wing of the Army-Corps, and will eventually be in a position 'to drive it away from the Passarge. How can the Detachment prevent him from doing that?

It is standing at Herzogswalde. The nature of the map makes it exceedingly difficult to judge the ground correctly. It took me some time before I got a clear idea of 'it. I estimate that Herzogswalde lies low at its southern part arid rises gently towards the north; it is commanded immediately on the south. The whole hilly ground between Herzogswalde and the Wuchsnig lake is very much confused. It consists of a number of knolls, which are separated by irregularly-formed and sometimes deep glens. Towards the patches of wood, the western part of which bears the name of Ponarien forest the ground slopes gently downwards, but then rises again to sink once more towards the former, but now drained, Bergling lake. In short, the ground on the whole is undulating; but even these undulations are very much mixed, and therefore difficult to use. Of prominent objects there are marked on the map: the Teufels Berg, which considerably commands all the rest of the ground; adjoining that Berg is something resembling a strongly-marked plateau, which gives me the impression that the Detachment could, in some measure, find a position there. It would of course have in front the strip of wood, and the question would therefore arise whether we should occupy it for defence or not. I would decide not to do so; it has the great advantage of partly hiding us from the enemy's view. If you imagine the Detachment to be posted on the plateau south of Herzogswalde, then the enemy cannot very well pass it by the highroad; he would lay himself open to an attack on his flank. The ground between Passarge and the line of little lakes is, moreover, rather narrow, and hardly large enough for the deployment of an Army-Corps.

The enemy could also determine to advance over the left plateau, thus aiming the blow at the Detachment. He would then, however, do only what we want: he would have to leave the Corps alone and to give up attacking it on that day; for we can count upon a considerable gain of time. The Detachment would then have to engage in a fight, and, if pressed, would withdraw in the direction of Alt Bolitten, in order to rejoin there the right wing of the Army-Corps.

The enemy will probably not adopt any of the possible courses hitherto mentioned, but try to advance over both sections of the ground. He will then be obliged to divide his forces, and to attack the Detachment in any case; for under no circumstances can he advance by Banners so long as the Detachment stands at Herzogswalde. By holding on to that position, the deployment of the Army-Corps is at all events secured, and so much time is probably gained that evening comes before the enemy can begin the attack.

On the whole, gentlemen have grasped in this instance the situation correctly. Differences, however, are apparent in the choice of the position in which the enemy is to be awaited. Some gentlemen advance as far as the strip of wood, in order to await the enemy there. Gentlemen, that strip of wood is almost 3½ miles long, and so of far too great an extent. In doing so, they almost seem to have an intention of drawing the enemy's special attention upon themselves. He will, however, not advance without reconnoitring. If he learns that any troops whatsoever are on his flank, he will naturally try to find out how strong they are. It surely is not necessary to make him particularly attentive. Some gentlemen have gone still further, and wish to deal short offensive blows. That does not look healthy. They move away from their Army-Corps in a manner not warranted, and with the only result that the enemy would throw himself upon them and annihilate them. The retreat must in all circumstances be made on the right wing of the Army-Corps. Some gentlemen have fixed the retreat on Liebstadt; that is not correct. We must keep the front of the Corps clear; otherwise we would place it perhaps in the position of being unable to cover even our retreat, and of still being itself attacked on that same day.

It was frequently omitted in the papers to take any notice of the Dragoon Regiment. It was standing at Seubersdorf or Waltersdorf, and will best make its retreat by the high-road, and then rejoin the Detachment by turning the Wuchsnig lake on the north. In an action it can hardly be used to any advantage. But at Waltersdorf it has the advantage of being able to overlook the whole advance of the enemy, and is in a position to hinder him from reconnoitring the Passarge downwards and getting a clear view of our situation.

The solution by the Field-Marshal once more summarised would therefore be:

FOR THE EVENING OF THE 1ST:

Bivouac between Langguther and Lobe lakes with few measures of security.

FOR THE 2ND:

Early start (6 o'clock), pushing out to the defile at Locken the Dragoon Regiment with a Battery, later on occupation of the positions there with the Main Body of the Detachment, advance of 2 Squadrons with 2 guns to Horn; next, more reconnoitring and watching until the enemy's intentions are more clearly discerned; eventually pushing forward the Detachment to Horn.

FOR THE 3RD:

Reconnaissance towards Deppen. Position of the Detachment somewhere south of Herzogswalde, in which a direct attack is to be awaited.

If the enemy should commit a mistake and advance by the highroad only, then an attempt to fall upon his left flank. I think that this will best be done past the north of the Wuchsnig lake. The Detachment would be in a position, if the enemy should attack with only a small fraction of his forces, to leave opposed to that, a small portion of its troops, and to strike on the enemy's flank with the remainder. If pressed, then retreat on the right wing of the Army-Corps. Considering the distances and the daylight, we can with certainty count upon the enemy not succeeding in forcing the Corps to give battle on that day.

In general I can say that gentlemen have had a correct conception, and that they have mostly also clearly developed it. The Field-Marshal is less concerned with your hitting off exactly what he wishes than with your developing your intentions in a clear manner. There are but few gentlemen whose papers must be considered a failure.

APPENDIX.

I.

DETAILS OF STRENGTH OF THE VARIOUS TACTICAL UNITS MENTIONED IN THE PROBLEMS, NOT ALWAYS APPARENT IN THE TEXT.

ONE REGIMENT OF INFANTRY = 3 Battalions, designated either 1st, 2nd, and 3rd, or 1st, 2nd, and Fusilier Battalions.

ONE BATTALION OF INFANTRY= 1,000 men in 4 Companies of 3 sections or Züge.

ONE RIFLE BATTALION ... = the same as Infantry.

ONE ENGINEER BATTALION ... = do.

ONE REGIMENT OF CAVALRY, where not otherwise stated, is 600 sabres in 4 Squadrons of 4 Züge or Troops each.

ONE BATTERY OF ARTILLERY, where not otherwise stated, has 6 guns.

THE OLD GERMAN 4-pr. is equivalent to an English 9-pr.

„ „ 8-pr. „ „ 16-pr.

„ „ 12-pr. „ „ 24-pr.

2.

VOCABULARY OF GERMAN TERMS USED IN THE TEXT, AND REFERRING TO THE MAP.—THE NUMBERS IN BRACKETS DENOTE THE PROBLEMS AND SOLUTIONS IN WHICH THEY OCCUR.

A.
Alt=old (11).
Alte=old (66).

B.
Bach=brook, stream, rivulet (26).
Berg=hill (3), (34), (66).
Berge=hills (50).
Braun=brown (4).
Bruch=bog, marsh, swampy meadows (3), (64).

C.
Chaussee Haus=turnpike, toll-house (6).

D.
Drei=three (53).

F.
Feld=field (59).
F. H. =Forsthaus=forester's house (42), (43).
Fichten=pines (51), (64).

Fliess=brook, stream (14), (53).
Fluth=flood (51).
Forst=forest, woods (51).
Forsthaus=forester's house (42), (53).
Fst. =Forst (vide it) (7).

G.
Geographische=geographical.
Graben=ditch (51).
Grube=pit (4).
Gr. =gross=great (52)
Grund=valley, dale, glen, bottom (3), (19).

H.
Haff=inlets of the Baltic near Danzig, Königsberg, and Memel (50).
Haus=house (6), (42), (53).
Heide=heath (64).
Heilige=holy (53).
Hinterste=hindmost (46), (47).
Hohen=high, tall (51).
Holz=wood, copse (59).

J.

Juden Kirchhof=Jews' cemetery (6).

K.

Kirchhof=cemetery, churchyard (6).
Kl. =Klein=little (11).
Kön. =Königlich=royal (4).
Kohlen=coals (4).

L.

Luch=bog, marsh, meadow (30).

M.

M.=Mühle=Mill (53), (65), (66).
Maasstab } scale.
Masstab }

N.

Nonnenbruch=nun's bog or marsh (43).

P.

Pfuhl=pond (53), (64).

R.

Rennsteig=drive (38), (39).
Römer=Roman (63).

S.

Schacht=shaft, pit, mine (55).
Schleuse=sluice-gate, lock (53).
Schritt=pace, step.
See=lake.
Steig=path (38), (39).
Strasse=road (63).

T.

Teich=pond (61), (65).
Tief=deep (3).

U.

Uebersichts-Skizzen=sketch-maps.
U. F.=Unter Försterei (53).
Unter-Försterei=gamekeeper's lodge (53).

V.

Vorstadt=suburb (48).
Vw. =Vorwerk=farm (9), (15), (39), (42), (53).

W.

Wasser=water, stream, brook, rivulet.
Weg=path, lane, road (61).

Z.

Zgl. =Ziegelei=brickfield (4), (64).

3.

EXPLANATION OF THE MARGINAL NOTES ON THE MAPS.

Masstab }
Maasstab } $\frac{1}{100000}$ der natürlichen Länge=natural scale $\frac{1}{100000}$.

PLANS I., IV., VII., IX., XIII., XIV., XV., XVI., XVIII., XX., XXI., XXIII., XXVI., XXVII., on right-hand bottom corner: "Die Zahlen geben," etc.=The numbers indicate the absolute heights in feet above the level of the Baltic. By the new measure 1,000 Prussian feet=376,62 metres.

PLAN II. On right-hand bottom corner: "Preussisches Gebiet," etc.=Prussian territory surveyed by the Royal Prussian General Staff, 1837-38.
Lippe territory according to the map published by the Lippe Government in 1887. Waldeck territory reconnoitred, 1889.
Corrections up to 1890.

PLAN VI. Left-hand bottom corner: "Die Höhenzahlen in," etc.=The heights in Austrian territory refer to the level of the Adriatic.

THIRD AND REVISED EDITION, ROYAL 8VO., 15s. NET.

MODERN TACTICS,

BY

CAPTAIN H. R. GALL

(LATE 5TH FUSILIERS).

This Edition has been almost rewritten, and contains upwards of 50 plates and numerous worked-out schemes, illustrating how to dispose of a Force in a map.

OPINIONS OF THE PRESS.

" Captain Gall's book will be of great value to military students going up for examination. His style is lucid and simple. The chapters upon reconnoitring and outpost duty are full, and of most useful character, and the whole question of attack and defence is treated with great ability. Lieutenant Eustace Balfour has contributed a useful chapter on cyclist infantry. The plates admirably illustrate the text."—*Army and Navy Gazette.*

" The book deals with the most recent developments of the art of war. It takes into account what perhaps are the most striking factors in the study of ' modern ' tactics—the ever narrowing margin between armed infantry and artillery fire, the increased range of both, and the consequent and paramount question of fire discipline ; and finally the indispensability of the spade as a military implement. Lieutenant Eustace Balfour has set forth clearly and conclusively the great possibilities of the cycle for military purposes in a country intersected by roads." —*Saturday Review.*

" Captain Gall has notably succeeded in his desire to present his teaching in a simple and easy form. One great recommendation of the work is that it takes cognisance of the most recent developments in the art of war—such, for example, as mounted infantry, machine guns, the increased range of modern artillery, and cyclist infantry. The chapter on the employment of cyclist infantry is from the pen of Lieutenant Eustace Balfour, and is pregnant with interest."—*Scotsman.*

" The style is clear and simple, and the explanations, helped as they are by numerous plans, will no doubt easily be grasped by those for whom they are written."—*Morning Post.*

" The work will be studied with much interest in this country, at the present time, when new manuals of tactics for our army are receiving so much attention." —*The Washington Army and Navy Register.*

" The method of instruction employed is extremely clear and concise, and is especially remarkable by the careful synopsis which the author has made of the most recent innovations in the military art, and the employment of the different arms. Among the rest is an extremely interesting chapter by Lieutenant Eustace Balfour on the employment of infantry mounted on velocipedes. The book has a much greater intrinsic value than that which the author ascribes to it. Young officers who are desirous of following the advances made almost daily by tactical science may read this book with advantage."—*Rivista Militare Italiana.*

London : **W. H. ALLEN & Co., Ltd., 13, Waterloo Place.**